Your Words YOUR STORY

ADD MEANINGFUL JOURNALING TO YOUR LAYOUTS

Michele**Skinner**

MEMORY
MAKERS
BOOKS

Cincinnati, Ohio

www.mycraftivity.com

IN THE AUTHOR'S WORDS

I have been a writer my entire life. Even when I dabbled in other areas, I would always come back to writing. When I found scrapbooking and realized that I could both write and express myself visually, I knew that the universe was sending me a glorious present! Being on design teams and getting published were never my focus, though I have been lucky enough to design for several web sites and have had work in *Paper Kuts, Ivy Cottage, Creating Keepsakes* and *Simple Scrapbooks*. My outlook on being published changed drastically in 2006 when, on a whim, I entered and won a spot on the 2007 Memory Makers Masters team. What a blessing! Without Memory Makers' belief in me and my work, you wouldn't be holding this book in your hands right now. My family and my love of words and photography are the main focus of my pages, and regardless of where I go now with this hobby, that focus will never change.

12 11 10 09 08   5 4 3 2 1

Distributed in Canada by Fraser Direct
100 Armstrong Avenue
Georgetown, ON, Canada L7G 5S4
Tel: (905) 877-4411

Distributed in the U.K. and Europe by David & Charles
Brunel House, Newton Abbot, Devon, TQ12 4PU, England
Tel: (+44) 1626 323200, Fax: (+44) 1626 323319
E-mail: postmaster@davidandcharles.co.uk

Distributed in Australia by Capricorn Link
P.O. Box 704, S. Windsor, NSW 2756 Australia
Tel: (02) 4577-3555

Library of Congress Cataloging-in-Publication Data

Skinner, Michele.
  Your words, your story : add meaningful journaling to your layouts / Michele Skinner. – 1st ed.
      p. cm.
  Includes index.
  ISBN 978-1-59963-027-4 (pbk. : alk. paper)
  1. Photograph albums. 2. Scrapbook journaling. 3. Scrapbooking. I. Title.
  TR501.S554 2008
  745.593–dc22

                      2008023366

Metric Conversion Chart

to convert	to	multiply by
Inches	Centimeters	2.54
Centimeters	Inches	0.4
Feet	Centimeters	30.5
Centimeters	Feet	0.03
Yards	Meters	0.9
Meters	Yards	1.1
Sq. Inches	Sq. Centimeters	6.45
Sq. Centimeters	Sq. Inches	0.16
Sq. Feet	Sq. Meters	0.09
Sq. Meters	Sq. Feet	10.8
Sq. Yards	Sq. Meters	0.8
Sq. Meters	Sq. Yards	1.2
Pounds	Kilograms	0.45
Kilograms	Pounds	2.2
Ounces	Grams	28.3
Grams	Ounces	0.035

fw

F+W PUBLICATIONS, INC.

Editor: Kristin Boys
Designer: Corrie Schaffeld
Art Coordinator: Eileen Aber
Production Coordinator: Matt Wagner
Photographers: Tim Grondin; John Carrico, Alias Imaging
Stylists: Nora Martini, Lauren Emmerling

DEDICATION

This is dedicated to Marc, who told me to write a book. And to Henry and Harper, who make life worth writing about.

ACKNOWLEDGMENTS

Thank you to Jess and Molly, who gave me those first few sheets of paper and stickers eight years ago and started me on this journey.

Thank you to my parents, who never told me to go outside and play when I shut myself in my room for hours, drawing and writing.

Thank you to my amazing editors and friends at F+W Publications: Christine, Kristin, Corrie, Eileen, Amy and the rest of the Memory Makers family. You are all so dear, and you know you'll never be rid of me!

Thank you to my crazy-talented contributors: Sue, Nisa, Sandra, Nicole, Catherine, Katrina, and Crystal. I am in awe of your talents and moved by your stories, but more importantly, I am so proud to call you all my friends!

Thank you to the scores of scrappers with whom I talked about journaling over the course of this project. Your open and honest answers inspired me, and your candid responses and concerns made me want to write the very best possible book for you. I hope in some small way this book will help you find ways to get your voice on the page.

And last, but not least, thank you to coffee, vodka and all the people I begged, bribed and paid to watch my children so I could write this book. Without your support and availability, this never would have gotten done almost on time.

TABLE OF CONTENTS

Marc and I were talking to Henry the other day, and one of the things we asked was, "What is your favorite thing to do?" Expecting him to answer Legos or video games or playing with friends, we were taken aback when he said, "Reading!"

I have to admit, I'm sort of surprised by how hard the reading bug has gripped him. Henry takes after Marc in so many ways, yet this reading thing ... that's all me! Who knew he would take to it so enthusiastically?

We always knew Henry was "gifted" ... those "Is Your Child Gifted and Talented?" lists always sound exactly like him. So I guess it shouldn't have been a surprise that he's a reader. But it was. One night when Henry was four, we were lying in his bed, reading bedtime stories, and he asked if he could read to us. And he did. He read the first page perfectly. He turned the page and read that one perfectly too. Marc and I just thought, well, we've read this book so many times that he has it memorized. To test our theory, we flipped to a random page in the middle of the book, and by golly if Henry didn't read THAT page perfectly!

When did he learn to read?!

Now, at nearly eight, Henry keeps stacks of books in progress on his dresser. And more on the floor. And looks forward to weekly library visits as if they were holidays. He zipped through the Lemony Snicket series, the Magic Tree House books were child's play, he devours books about science and nature and pirates and spies, and he is currently engrossed in "Black Beauty." And "The Adventures of Tom Sawyer" is on deck.

Amazing.

I love that he loves to read. Books will take him anywhere he wants to go in life. And I hope it's a passion that continues to grow in him, if for no other reason than it gives us something in common. Taking him to the library or bookstore is such a fun experience.

Besides, I have a feeling Marc gets everything else.

HE'S A rEaDer

5 years later

I woke up today and the weather, fittingly and thankfully, is gray and cold and gloomy. I'm not sure how people would feel if it was warm and gorgeous today. Like it was then.

It's inevitable that we instinctively think back to where we were at any given minute of that day five years ago, and all that disbelief is made fresh.

I still can't watch shows and news about September 11th without feeling a total sense of astonishment. And while I wasn't personally affected, Marc's uncle lost two business partners on one of the first planes. And his boss was in the Marriott at the base of the World Trade Center that morning and had to evacuate with the clothes on his back. Peripheral, but still sobering.

That morning our cable was out, so Henry and I were just playing and taking our time getting ready for the day. When Marc called to say a plane had crashed into the Trade Center, like most people I believed it to be some small plane. I immediately thought, "Oh - those poor people!" thinking about those on the affected floors and the firemen who would have to attempt to rescue them. My dad was a fireman for most of my life ... I know the gear they carry and can't imagine having to lug it dozens of flights of stairs and *then* fight a massive fire.

When Marc called a few minutes later, though, to report the second plane, the journalist in me knew this wasn't a random incident. There's no way it could happen twice accidentally. And suddenly I was pissed off that I didn't have access to CNN. I ran upstairs with Henry, stuck him in front of a video, and tried in vain to get online to see what was going on. But all the news sites were overloaded and nothing worked.

I called my friend Heather to see if we could go to her house to watch and she said of course. On the way there, I listened on the radio as the first tower fell and I felt like being sick. I called Marc, at work in a tall financial building downtown, and told him to come to Heather's. I didn't want him at work. He said people were already being told to leave the building. Through the stairways.

Together, the three of us watched the second tower fall. And heard about the Pentagon. And the plane in Pennsylvania.

I was so afraid for the future my son would have. He was only 18 months old and I was worried that he would grow up in a world devoid of trust, innocence, peace.

Today, five years later, I still worry about that. Especially since he is a boy. What lies ahead of him? More wars to fight?

And now I have a daughter, who is, ironically, 17 months old. She will never know a world pre-9.11. She was brought into a world that was in full knowledge of the terror and hate and evil that lurks. What will she see in her lifetime? I shudder to think what her "9.11" will be. Worse than the one five years ago? Quite probably. That scares the out of me.

As a parent, all you want for your kids is their happiness and safety. Was it selfish of to have another child, knowing the world into which we were bringing her? Or having her our sign of hope, our prayer for peace?

There are still so many questions, but today I pray for families who lost loved ones, the ones who were lost, for the ones who survived, for the ones still fighting, for us all

9.11.06

HONOR

wHy thIs plac

There's just something about the North Shore. Maybe because it's at the same latitude as Maine, a place I love. Maybe because it has pure elemental features — rocks, trees, water — and not much else. Maybe because the dress code is a sweatshirt and hiking boots. Maybe because all I have to do is listen to the waves crash or the rivers rush or the aspens whisper. Maybe because it lacks traffic or Target or cell phone coverage. Maybe because I can breathe freely and deeply and without having to be reminded. Maybe because when I drive up into the Arrowhead and see Lake Superior out the window, I feel as *home* there as I've felt anywhere in my life. Whatever the reason, no matter where I travel in my life and where I may live, the North Shore will always pull me as strongly as a magnetic pole. It is my true North.

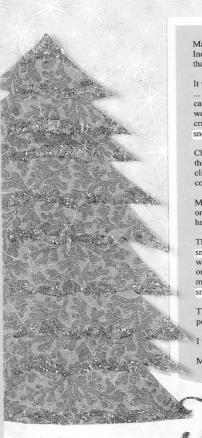

Marc and I got engaged on December 23, 1995, and on December 24th he drove down to Indianapolis to be with his family. That evening, it started to snow. It was that quiet, perfect snow that makes you feel like you're inside a snow globe.

It was so perfect that my entire family - parents, sister, grandparents, aunts and uncles and cousins ... all 15 of us - bundled up and headed out. My grandparents lived on a lake at the edge of a college campus, so off we all trudged around the lake, visiting professors and faculty who lived nearby so we could carol them. We returned to the house full of holiday spirit and ready to drink hot cocoa, crack nuts on the hearth, eat Chex mix, and do all of our Christmas Eve traditions. And watch the snow fall.

Christmas morning came, the world was white, and the snow was still falling. We opened gifts, and the snow started to come down harder. It was warm enough that the flakes were fat and sticky and clinging to everything. By lunchtime, snow covered all the trees, and it was falling so hard that we couldn't see across the lake.

My college roommate was at her in-laws' house down the road, and she called to congratulate me on the engagement and invited me over so she could see my ring. I laced up my boots, put on my hat and mittens, and off I went.

The snow was so thick that I could hear it falling; the world was in complete white-out, and the snow was up to my knees. There were no cars and no noise anywhere, except the yells of some kids who were sledding. I was in a sheer state of bliss, but I didn't know if it was from the amazing snow or the diamond on my finger and thought that this time next year I would be married to the love of my life. And I wished so badly that Marc could have been there to share this incredible Christmas snow with me.

The walk was actually tiring because I had to trudge through the deep, heavy snow, but it was perfect. It was like Norman Rockwell and Thomas Kincaid and Currier & Ives all rolled together.

I want a snow like that every single year. And I never want to experience it without Marc again.

Maybe that's why we moved to Minnesota.

The Perfect Snow

romances, and finding tru...

...e months of sitting by each other i...
...ng more familiar with each other...
...y liked this Marc guy. She talked to...
... is now dating Rollin. Marc's...
...ichele to call Marc, because he was...
...han computers and basketball, and...
...him to ask out anyone. Michele...
...n to a floor-activity hockey game,...
...t April. Marc said, "Okay." They...
...ele was non-plussed. She tried...
...loor activity at the skating rink?"...
...d a better time.

...to spend more time together.
...asses and talked afterward. They...
...r meals. But it never progressed,...
... longer worth the effort.

...home one night and told Michele, "There's this boy in my class. He's not much of a talker, and he's from somewhere in South America, but his name is Marc, and you two would make the most beautiful babies." Michele rolled her eyes.

- 1992, Fall. Michele decided, against her better judgment, to attend the local college. While at the street party on the eve of the school year, she bumped into her friend, Rollin. He asked her, "Have you met my roommate, Marc?" Michele and Marc looked at each other, and both remembered meeting at the dining commons the previous year. They said hello. The boys walked away, and Michele walked away with her friend.

- 1993, Winter. Michel and Marc have been friends for several months. They hung out with the same people and ate meals at the same table. One day in January, proverbial lightning hit Michele and she realized, "Hey ... this is a pretty cute guy. And he's actually nice. Huh." She began to obsess. And Marc began to sit by Michele in Sociology class.

 true

true Story

 love

...le had plans to go to Myrtle ...each for the week. The day she was to leave, the phone rang. It was Marc, and he asked her to go play pool at the HUB. Surprised and pleased, Michele said, "Okay." They played pool for more than an hour, and then Michele had to leave to meet her friend and catch a Greyhound.

That night, there was a blizzard in Kentucky and the bus company canceled the trip.

Two days later, Michele bumped into Rollin and he told her Marc was home and bored, and suggested Michele call. So she did. That very day. And asked Marc if he wanted to get ice cream. He said, "Okay." They had a lovely time, and decided to meet the next morning at the college gym.

The next day, Marc and Michele had a wonderful time together. Hours flew by, and Marc admitted that he got the nerve to call Michele before spring break because he realized he would miss her and didn't want her to forget about him while she was gone. Michele smiled.

Marc walked Michele to the fine arts building where her mom worked. They walked into her office and Michele introduced Marc to her mom. Her mom looked at Marc, looked at Michele, and dragged Michele into the utility closet. "That's Handsome Marc! From my class!" Michele's mom said.

In that instant, Michele knew that she would be with Marc forever.

WHAT ABOUT THE STORY?

I got into scrapbooking because I needed a baby book for my son that fit my style—no cartoon characters, no "perfect" family tree, no cliché pastels. In the beginning, scrapping was mostly about getting photos down on pretty paper and adding a clever title, but then one day it hit me that this was my opportunity to tell my children the stories of their lives.

Scrapbooking is, of course, about the photos and the paper. But what about the story? What do our children get from all the hours and money we spend on pages? We want them to know who they are, who we are, what life is like. I imagine my kids will quickly turn past pages that have a cute portrait photo, lots of arty embellishments, and a beautiful title or quote. The pages that will really grab their attention will be the ones that tell a story. I wish my own family had done that. To read my mother's thoughts of me when I was a child would be priceless.

Yet for many scrappers, writing is the most uncomfortable and hardest part to accomplish. For many people, writing does not come easily. They think they need to write the "right" way. Or journaling comes out flat because they can't find their own voice—the words that make the story reflect their personality.

For me, writing has always come easily, so that's where I place the emphasis on my scrapbook pages. Yes, I love photography. Yes, I love playing with product. But the words … ahh! Those are the soul of the page. You should feel privileged to put your soul down on paper, not afraid of it. But how is it done? In this book, I give you permission to explore your voice. Follow my prompts to see just how authentic your writing voice is. Read through the Problem Solved features scattered throughout the chapters. They offer real-life solutions for those pesky problems that keep you from telling your story. Try on different writing styles and practice with a new form of journaling. See what fits. Different pages will call for different styles of journaling, and I want you to know that it's OK to play with words and make them do what you want them to do.

I hope you find nuggets of inspiration in the pages and stories shared here. I hope something nudges you and says, "Hey! You have a story like this! Go write it down!" I hope you find your voice and love its sound.

You and elizabeth found this caterpillar in our garden. we put "her" in the bug box. You fed "her" a lot of milkweed. She got fat. made her crysalis. 14 days later...

a BEAUTIFUL butterfly emerged. AMAZING!

CHANGE

june 2007

eva, change can lead to some BEAUTIFUL things...embrace change! mom

8

PART 1
Your Words
FIND THEM!

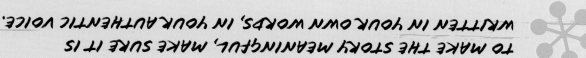

W e all struggle with journaling, but why is that? Is it because it's the most time-consuming part? Is it because we lack confidence using our handwriting? Is it because we feel we won't get the story across in a way that will be interesting?

There are many different reasons why we avoid journaling, but what we forget is that our scrapbooks can actually have a purpose giving us a creative outlet! They are our way of showing our family how much they mean to us, how much they make us laugh, how much they make us think. Scrapbooks are our way of telling their story, our own story, and any other story. The key, though, is to make the story meaningful to anyone who reads it, and the surest way of accomplishing that is to make sure the story is written in our own words, in our authentic voice.

Wait . . . what? What is an authentic voice?

Authentic voice is the voice we use when we are being 100 percent ourselves, without fear or reservation. Think about the person you are when you're with your friends, your spouse or significant other, your children, and your family. This is your authentic voice. When you create a scrapbook for those you love, your self and voice should come through loud and clear. Is that something you're already doing, or is it the one part of scrapping that still stumps you?

Here's a little quiz to see where you fall on the journaling spectrum:

1. Do you have scrapbook pages that have gone unfinished for days, months, even years because you can't get the journaling started?

2. Do you find yourself doing pages for the sake of art rather than posterity because the idea of journaling is so unattractive?

3. Do you avoid holiday and event pages because the journaling is the same year after year? Or do you do holiday and event pages only because you don't have to think about the journaling?

4. Do you use quotes and lyrics for pages rather than your own words because you feel there is no way you could say it better?

5. Does your journaling read flat because you are trying to write information rather than observations?

6. Does your journaling have a cheesy tone because you are trying to write with heartfelt emotions but it ends up sounding forced and unnatural?

If you answered yes to any of these questions, this is the book for you. Now, let's go find your voice. Once you find it, you can really start to use it!

TO MAKE THE STORY MEANINGFUL, MAKE SURE IT IS WRITTEN IN YOUR OWN WORDS, IN YOUR AUTHENTIC VOICE.

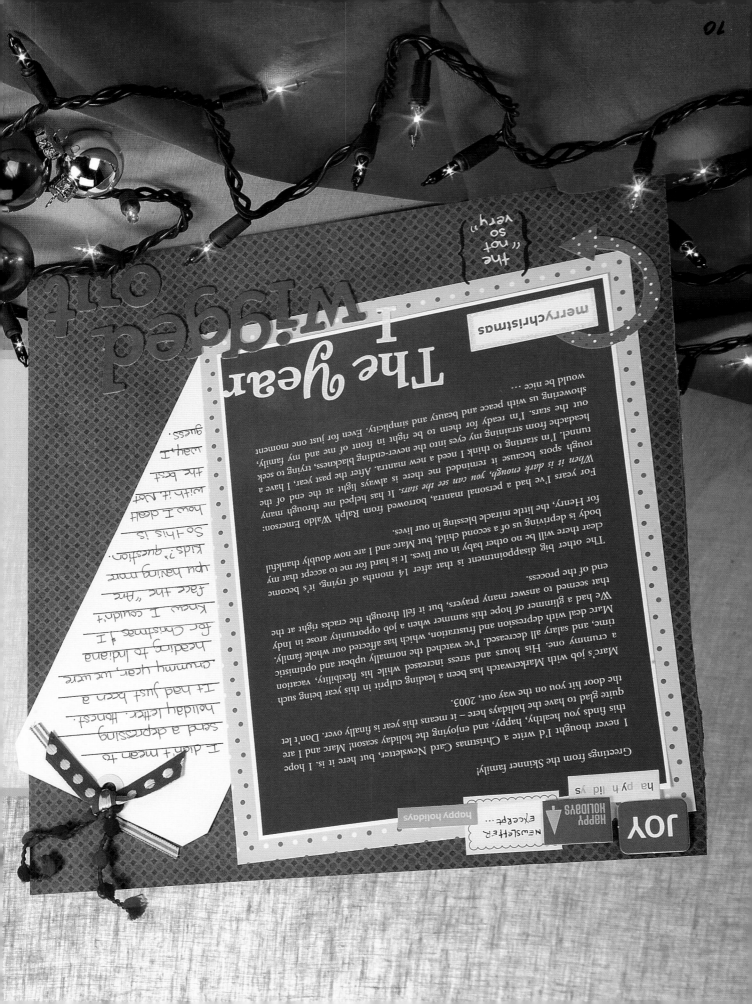

The Year I Wiggled Out

the "not so very"

merrychristmas

Greetings from the Skinner family!

I never thought I'd write a Christmas Card Newsletter, but here it is. I hope this finds you healthy, happy, and enjoying the holiday season! Marc and I are quite glad to have the holidays here – it means this year is finally over. Don't let the door hit you on the way out, 2003.

Marc's job with Marketwatch has been a leading culprit in this year being such a crummy one. His hours and stress increased while his flexibility, vacation time, and salary all decreased. I've watched the normally upbeat and optimistic Marc deal with depression and frustration, which has affected our whole family. We had a glimmer of hope this summer when a job opportunity arose in Indy that seemed to answer many prayers, but it fell through the cracks right at the end of the process.

The other big disappointment is that after 14 months of trying, it's become clear there will be no other baby in our lives. It is hard for me to accept that my body is depriving us of a second child, but Marc and I are now doubly thankful for Henry, the little miracle blessing in our lives.

For years I've had a personal mantra, borrowed from Ralph Waldo Emerson: *When it is dark enough, you can see the stars.* It has helped me through many rough spots because it reminded me there is always light at the end of the tunnel. I'm starting to think I need a new mantra. After the past year, I have a headache from straining my eyes into the never-ending blackness, trying to seek out the stars. I'm ready for them to be right in front of me and my family, showering us with peace and beauty and simplicity. Even for just one moment would be nice …

I didn't mean to send a depressing holiday letter. Honest. It had just been a crummy year, we were heading to Indiana for Christmas & I knew I couldn't face the "Are you having more kids?" question. So this is how I dealt with it. Not the best way, I guess.

JOY

HAPPY HOLIDAYS

NEWSLETTER EXCERPT…

happy holidays

ha p y h lid y s

USING YOUR OWN WORDS

How do you discover if you are using your authentic voice? Think of how you speak on the phone, the voice you use when typing an e-mail, or the words you choose when telling a story at the dinner table. Does that voice match the voice you use when you write journaling on a scrapbook page?

Let's do a little exercise. Think of a recent scrapbook page you created. Think of the memory or the story behind it. Now, call your mom or best friend or child and tell them the story. Here's how you can start: "Hey, remember when . . . ?" or, "Did I ever tell you about the time . . . ?" Once you finish that conversation, go find the scrapbook page and read it. Ask yourself if the voice with which you just told the story matches the voice with which the story is written. If they match, great! You know how to use your authentic voice. If they're quite different, well, read on!

There is no better place to start getting to the authentic heart of the story than your own blog entries and e-mails. They are already written and ready to go; just copy, paste and scrap! The nice thing about using blog entries or sent mail is that typically they are written in a timely fashion to the event. That is to say, the words and emotions are fresh because they are written while the topic is still on your mind and the true emotion is there.

DOES THE VOICE YOU USE AT THE DINNER TABLE MATCH THE VOICE YOU USE WHEN YOU WRITE JOURNALING ON A SCRAPBOOK PAGE?

Supplies: Patterned paper (BoBunny, Heidi Grace); letter stickers (American Crafts, Making Memories); holiday stickers (Making Memories); tag (Anchor Paper); bracket stamp (7gypsies); pens (Sharpie, Uniball); Misc: ribbon

BLOGS

Using blog entries as a starting point for journaling helps you incorporate your authentic voice into a page.

5 years later

I woke up today and the weather, fittingly and thankfully, is gray and cold and gloomy. I'm not sure how people would feel if it was warm and gorgeous today. Like it was then.

It's inevitable that we instinctively think back to where we were at any given minute of that day five years ago, and all that disbelief is made fresh.

I still can't watch shows and news about September 11th without feeling a total sense of astonishment. And while I wasn't personally affected, Marc's uncle lost two business partners on one of the first planes. And his boss was in the Marriott at the base of the World Trade Center that morning and had to evacuate with the clothes on his back. Peripheral, but still sobering.

That morning our cable was out, so Henry and I were just playing and taking our time getting ready for the day. When Marc called to say a plane had crashed into the Trade Center, like most people I believed it to be some small plane. I immediately thought, "Oh - those poor people!" thinking about those on the affected floors and the firemen who would have to attempt to rescue them. My dad was a fireman for most of my life ... I know the gear they carry and can't imagine having to lug it dozens of flights of stairs and *then* fight a massive fire.

When Marc called a few minutes later, though, to report the second plane, the journalist in me knew this wasn't a random incident. There's no way it could happen twice accidentally. And suddenly I was pissed off that I didn't have access to CNN. I ran upstairs with Henry, stuck him in front of a video, and tried in vain to get online to see what was going on. But all the news sites were overloaded and nothing worked.

I called my friend Heather to see if we could go to her house to watch and she said of course. On the way there, I listened on the radio as the first tower fell and I felt like being sick. I called Marc, at work in a tall financial building downtown, and told him to come to Heather's. I didn't want him at work. He said people were already being told to leave the building. Through the stairways.

Together, the three of us watched the second tower fall. And heard about the Pentagon. And the plane in Pennsylvania.

I was so afraid for the future my son would have. He was only 18 months old and I was worried that he would grow up in a world devoid of trust, innocence, peace.

Today, five years later, I still worry about that. Especially since he is a boy. What lies ahead of him? More wars to fight?

And now I have a daughter, who is, ironically, 17 months old. She will never know a world pre-9.11. She was brought into a world that was in full knowledge of the terror and hate and evil that lurks. What will she see in her lifetime? I shudder to think what her "9.11" will be. Worse than the one five years ago? Quite probably. That scares the crap out of me.

As a parent, all you want for your kids is their happiness and safety. Was it selfish of us to have another child, knowing the world into which we were bringing her? Or was having her our sign of hope, our prayer for peace?

There are still so many questions, but today I pray for families who lost loved ones, for the ones who were lost, for the ones who survived, for the ones still fighting, for us all.

HONOR   9.11.06

Many bloggers use events as starting points for reminiscing. In that same fashion, I created this page around journaling I wrote on the fifth anniversary of 9/11, on a day that my son, Henry, was waiting for the bus and I was struck by how different the air felt five years later. I included a "Where I was when ..." narrative because it sets up the comparison, but the journaling is also a reflection on how things have changed in five years. As a nod to the event, I added two vertical columns on the page; visual symbolism is a great way to give strength to your words.

Supplies: Cardstock (Bazzill); patterned paper (KI Memories, My Mind's Eye); brads, letter stickers (Doodlebug); chipboard and rub-on accents (BasicGrey); word accent (Me & My Big Ideas); Misc: Times New Roman font, label holder

the **Quotable**

HENRY nO. 72

While driving to some friends' house for dinner on Sunday, Henry wanted to pretend our SUV was the Millenium Falcon. He's obsessed with Star Wars, if I haven't mentioned.

His words to us:

"Daddy, you be Han Solo. Mommy, you be Princess Leia. And Harper ... you can be Chewbacca."

Visions of how Henry will "play" with his little sister now dancing scarily in my head.

journaled july '05 · photo taken december '06

My son is full of zingers, and I try to write down everything so that I can create a book full of "Henry quotes." What your children do and say, or how they play and what their interests are, are great places to start your journaling on a layout. When my daughter is five, will her 10-year-old brother still be telling her to be Chewbacca? Well, yeah … that might happen. And if it does, this page is all the more poignant because it shows where it started.

Supplies: Cardstock (Bazzill, WorldWin); patterned paper (Wübie); letter stickers (Doodlebug, KI Memories); chipboard (Making Memories); Misc: 2 Peas Favorite Things and Century Gothic fonts

This was one of those blog entries that I had to type immediately after the conversation took place. I was typing through laughter, trying to get across my amusement at how geeky my husband is. It's a badge he wears proudly, but there are times when it strikes me that he isn't just of the nine-to-five variety. Have you captured someone's essence in a blog entry, or have you poked fun at someone's idiosyncrasies or traits? Blogs are a great place to look for blurbs about the quirks in the people around us.

Supplies: Cardstock (Bazzill, WorldWin); patterned paper (Piggy Tales); chipboard letters (Heidi Swapp); chipboard accents (Heidi Grace, Scenic Route, Technique Tuesday); brads (American Crafts); epoxy stickers (Cloud 9); Misc: Myriad Pro font

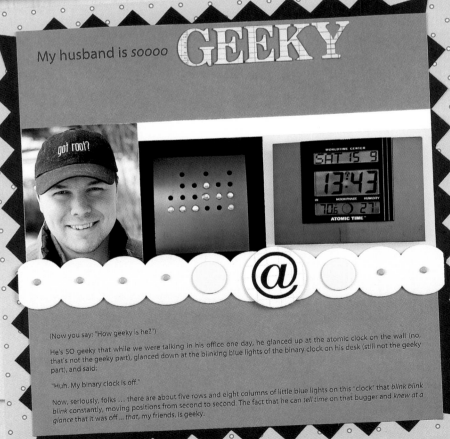

My husband is *soooo* GEEKY

(Now you say: "How geeky is he?")

He's SO geeky that while we were talking in his office one day, he glanced up at the atomic clock on the wall (no, that's not the geeky part), glanced down at the blinking blue lights of the binary clock on his desk (still not the geeky part), and said:

"Huh. My binary clock is off."

Now, seriously, folks … there are about five rows and eight columns of little blue lights on this "clock" that *blink blink blink* constantly, moving positions from second to second. The fact that he can *tell time* on that bugger and *knew at a glance* that it was off … *that,* my friends, is geeky.

PROBLEM SOLVED

"I want my words to sound real, but when I try to write like I talk, the structure is bad. How can I write in an authentic way and still write well?"

Do the grammar police hang out at your house? If not, write in a way that makes you happy! Or in a way that sounds like you. Or in a way that tells the story in the way you want to tell it. On this layout, I used vertical columns as a way to keep the story flowing through the series of photos. And the journaling reflects my way of telling the events of the day. Sometimes there are paragraphs that describe what was happening, but other times there are little comments for the photos that serve no purpose other than to be silly. But it all goes with the main point of the page. Are you sarcastic? Do you inject your humor into your observations? Do you tend to use run-on sentences? Then feel free to write the same way! I promise I won't take a red pen to your journaling, and no one else will, either.

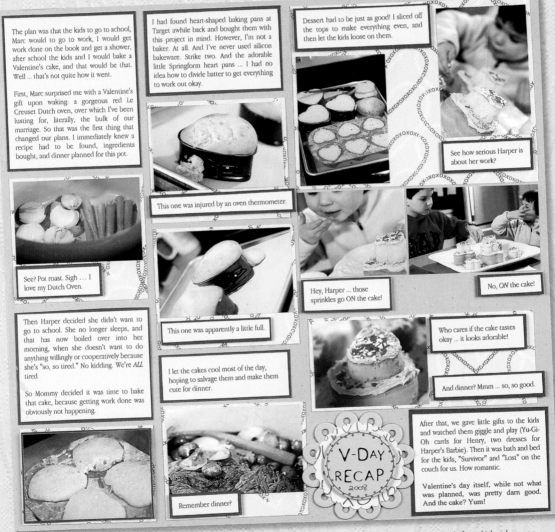

The plan was that the kids to go to school, Marc would to go to work, I would get work done on the book and get a shower, after school the kids and I would bake a Valentine's cake, and that would be that. Well ... that's not quite how it went.

First, Marc surprised me with a Valentine's gift upon waking: a gorgeous red Le Creuset Dutch oven, over which I've been lusting for, literally, the bulk of our marriage. So that was the first thing that changed our plans. I immediately knew a recipe had to be found, ingredients bought, and dinner planned for this pot.

I had found heart-shaped baking pans at Target awhile back and bought them with this project in mind. However, I'm not a baker. At all. And I've never used silicon bakeware. Strike two. And the adorable little Springform heart pans ... I had no idea how to divide batter to get everything to work out okay.

Dessert had to be just as good! I sliced off the tops to make everything even, and then let the kids loose on them.

See how serious Harper is about her work?

See? Pot roast. Sigh ... I love my Dutch Oven.

This one was injured by an oven thermometer.

Hey, Harper ... those sprinkles go ON the cake!

No, ON the cake!

Then Harper decided she didn't want to go to school. She no longer sleeps, and that has now boiled over into her morning, when she doesn't want to do anything willingly or cooperatively because she's "so, so tired." No kidding. We're ALL tired.

So Mommy decided it was time to bake that cake, because getting work done was obviously not happening.

This one was apparently a little full.

I let the cakes cool most of the day, hoping to salvage them and make them cute for dinner.

Who cares if the cake tastes okay ... it looks adorable!

And dinner? Mmm ... so, so good.

Remember dinner?

V-DAY RECAP 2008

After that, we gave little gifts to the kids and watched them giggle and play (Yu-Gi-Oh cards for Henry, two dresses for Harper's Barbie). Then it was bath and bed for the kids, "Survivor" and "Lost" on the couch for us. How romantic.

Valentine's day itself, while not what was planned, was pretty darn good. And the cake? Yum!

Supplies: Cardstock (Bazzill); patterned paper (Cloud 9, Pebbles); rub-on letters (Autumn Leaves); pen (Sharpie); Misc: Apple Garamond Light font, chipboard

1:30 p.m. on a Friday.

Harper's supposed to be napping, right? So when I hear her running around upstairs, I go take a look. And what do I see? Little Miss, in her Ariel jammies, wearing a pink ballet-flat-type slipper on one foot and a two-sizes-too-small pink fluffy slipper with pom poms on the other foot, crown on her head, and two different dress-up heels in her hands. And she says to me, with a big smile on her face:

"Mama, I wear crown for night-night?"

Then:

"Mama, I sleep in slippers! Like Strawberry Shortcake Sweet Dreams! I wear slippers. Crown, too?"

Now, her mastery of the English language leaves a lot to be desired most days, but her level of cuteness certainly does not.

Too bad the camera wasn't handy. Though I didn't feel like telling her to hold on, getting the camera, taking a pic, and *THEN* trying to explain why she couldn't do what she was doing during nap time. How do you criticize something that just made you smile and take a photo??

Gosh, she's cute.

i blog

because of stories like this.

Blogs can be a wonderful tool for creating a picture of something you weren't able to capture on film. There is no rule that says you have to use actual photos on a page. If a picture is worth a thousand words, I bet you can use a hundred or so to bring a mental image to life. On this day when my daughter was so cute, I didn't dare take a photo to encourage what she was doing. So on this layout I just explained why "I Blog."

Supplies: Cardstock (Bazzill); patterned paper (BoBunny, Collage Press); letter stickers (Heidi Grace); sticker accents (BoBunny); brads (Doodlebug); Misc: Lucida Bright and Wendy Medium fonts

When we blog or write in a journal, we tend to write our initial thoughts about a subject. But we don't always write the whole story, or sometimes the whole story doesn't unfold until later. If a story is meaningful to you, scrap it and make it complete! That's just what Nisa did here. She took a photo and wrote a short, witty blog entry about it. But after time, she came up with a deeper perspective on the topic and addressed it in this layout

Supplies: Patterned paper (Cross My Heart, Karen Foster); stickers (7gypsies); stamps (Purple Onion); brads (Making Memories); decorative punch (Marvy); Misc: notebook paper

Artwork by Nisa Fiin

sometimes...

sometimes a photo just gets it. magically captures what you see in a person. what you love about a person. sure there are the smiling photos of our loved ones that we all adore...but when it captures them just... being...it's amazing.

I am frantically in love with this photo of this boy I am frantically in love with. doesn't get much more magically delicious than that.

www.shootingstars

May 31, 2006 at 04:15 PM | Permalink

FIELD NOTES

This is the story behind the story. And this is what I need to remember. This is not the photo I meant to take. I just called his name and he looked back and I was hoping he would do something fantastic. But he didn't. He just was. He just looked back and was. And I thought - "Gee, thanks. Way to make a great photo. I'll delete that puppy later. Now let's go over here and take some "real" photos, ok?" Thankfully, I didn't delete it... Because it is one of my favorite photos of Ben of all time. Ever. It's genius. In just his being. And this is what I need to remember. Relax Nisa. Don't force it. Don't "make" the moments. Let them happen. Photograph your life. This is where the true magic is.

Photograph your life. Photograph your life. Photograph your life. Photograph your life.

LETTERS & E-MAILS

Whether they're words you've already written or thoughts you've never let out, letters to others (and yourself!) will infuse pages with your own voice.

To say that you screwed up one of the most important days of our lives is putting it, shall we say, *lightly*.

I understand that you had to retain your moral high ground, your "I'll never tell a lie" value system, but you couldn't have just let it go for 24 hours in order to avoid years of resentment?

Yes, you say you were young, that you didn't know how to do it the right way. But come on … that's a cop out. Men all over the world and of all ages propose to their girlfriends every day, and I bet it's only a small percentage who truly don't know what to do to such a degree that they screw it up and make their intended cry.

And not in the good way.

Yes, I misled you. I withheld the fact that Sandra and I went to the jeweler's to look at the ring because I wanted to spare YOU; I didn't want to ruin any surprise you may have cooked up for me. If only I'd known what would happen, I would have flat-out said, "Yup, we stopped in. But the ring wasn't there. Bummer." That would have saved you from having to trap me in my white lie to prove how morally corrupt *I* was and how honest and good *you* are. And thus it would have saved my one shot at being proposed to from the abysmal fate of being one of the biggest disappointments of my life.

But it's okay. Over the past eleven years I've worked on you. You are a better man in the sense that you still aren't all that romantic or overly thoughtful or sensitive, but at least you know better than to try and pull one over on me. Because ultimately, trying to out-moral me will come back to bite you in the backside. Repeatedly.

So I say that first proposal is your Take One. You will get another chance. I don't expect roses or skywriting or some elaborate scheme. I just expect what every girl wants: the man of her dreams, expressing his deepest love in the most sincere way, and leaving all that "I told you so" crap for a more appropriate time.

" WILL YOU MARRY ME? " : Take One

I have never actually written this letter to my husband, but this layout serves as the one I would write. His proposal was the antithesis of what I thought it should be . . . and believe me, he's heard about it! Take the opportunity to write letters to people regardless of whether or not they'll ever read them. You didn't get the chance to say what was in your heart? You thought of a great rebuttal after the fact? Time has changed your views? Write a letter.

Supplies: Cardstock (Bazzill, It Takes Two, WorldWin); patterned paper (KI Memories); ribbon (Paper Source); rhinestones (Mark Richards); iron-on thread (Kreinik); Misc: Apple Garamond Light and Gilligan's Island fonts

PRESSURE!

SCHOOL
CHORES
home WORK
dance

Sometimes it may seem that I don't understand the pressure you are feeling. School, chores, homework, dance ... it all weighs on you pretty heavy sometimes. You like to remind us that it's much worse for a twelve-year-old than for a grown-up. After all, we only have to go to work and then we're done for the day while your obligations continue until bedtime. Don't worry, Peanut. I do understand how hard it is to be twelve. While I can tell you that it will get easier, I know that won't help right now. So just know that I understand the pressure you are under. I want you to let me know if it ever feels like it's getting to be too much for you to handle because I will always be there for you while you figure this all out.

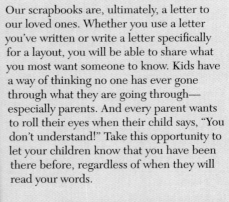

Our scrapbooks are, ultimately, a letter to our loved ones. Whether you use a letter you've written or write a letter specifically for a layout, you will be able to share what you most want someone to know. Kids have a way of thinking no one has ever gone through what they are going through—especially parents. And every parent wants to roll their eyes when their child says, "You don't understand!" Take this opportunity to let your children know that you have been there before, regardless of when they will read your words.

Supplies: Cardstock; patterned paper (Crate Paper); letter stickers (BasicGrey, Mustard Moon); stamp (PSX); brad, chipboard flower (Making Memories); Misc: Times New Roman font, ink, paint

Artwork by Sue Thomas

Education. This is big on your mind right now. You really want to go to Northland College on the edge of Lake Superior in Wisconsin. You really want to study environmental journalism and go work for Greenpeace. The last thing you want to do is end up at Huntington College. Let me just tell you that Northland would be awesome, and you will always wonder what you missed by not going. But let me also add that some pretty amazing things come out of your years at Huntington (coughcoughtheloveofyourlifecoughcough) ... don't knock it just yet.

I will add, though, that you need to relax a little in college and enjoy those four years. You will be so focused on getting out and getting away that you'll forget to really soak in the experience.

And when you meet a preppy little blonde across the hall freshman year, don't assume anything about her. She will turn out to be the most kindred friend you've ever had.

Career. I would recommend you follow your heart and pursue art and photography, but I know you won't. You'll assume that a high-powered career in public relations is what you want. So be it ... some good things will come of it.

However, I have one nugget of advice that will enable you to avoid one of the biggest regrets you'll have. When Mr. Karwoski himself invites you to do an unpaid internship with Karwoski & Courage in 1997, do not assume that because you had a by-line in Huntington, Indiana you are better than an internship. This is how big agencies in big cities work; you are a Nobody until you prove yourself over a few years. Take the freaking internship. Who knows what could come from it!!

Love. You are currently in the throes of your first love and all is wonderful. But you already know he's not the guy for you, and you will wisely break it off in a few months. It will hurt you to the core and you will think of him often over the years, but you know you want out. You are envisioning a guy with longish hair, a kayak strapped to the roof of his car, a wicked sense of humor, Birkenstocks, and some Thoreau stashed in his backpack, and you are off to find that person.

Just to let you know, halfway through your freshman year of college you will stumble upon a tall, lovely computer science major in turquoise wind pants and a Chicago Bulls jacket and you will be irretrievably lost to him forever, regardless of the "dream guy" vision in your head. But trust me ... it'll be a good move. Your life will be better than anything you've imagined about Kayak Boy. Just don't accept his first proposal ... make him do it the right way before you say yes.

Motherhood: It will happen earlier than you anticipate, but that's okay. One word of warning, though: after your first child is born, please please please seek help for post-partum depression. It will spiral out of control until one day, nine months later, you'll wake up and realize you have no memories of your child's life.

Don't fight with a baby who doesn't want to nurse – the guilt will wrack you and ignite the problem. Please take care of yourself and let others help. And when four years later there is no second baby yet, don't mourn. There is another child on the horizon, just not on the timetable you determine. Relax. Have faith. Don't despair. Your family will be complete very, very soon.

Self: Right now you have a hot little body. Enjoy it and appreciate it, and for the love of all things Size 7, respect it. You will soon have desk jobs, a near nervous breakdown, and dinners on you husband's expense account. And then you'll have kids. Fifteen years from now, you will not recognize yourself and it will depress you to no end. Maintaining five pounds is a whole lot easier than trying to shed the equivalent of a second-grader after years of ignoring what's happening. Trust me on that. Oh, and about following your heart into art and photography? A day will come when you will do just that. And you'll be happy.

from me   ... to you

Hi there, Michele-at-18. It's me – Michele-15-Years-Later. I know you're feeling unsure about many things, so I want to hand down a little advice, hindsight being 20/20 and all. There are several big areas that need to be addressed, so let's get started, shall we?

Most of us wish we could have known the future before making decisions. You can't go back in time, but you can write a letter to your younger self. Tell your five-year-old counterpart not to grab that hot pan. Warn your high school self to stay away from a group of friends. Encourage yourself as a young adult. Scrapbooks can be just as much about personal growth as they are memory preservation. And when we are being honest with ourselves, our real voice comes through.

Supplies: Cardstock (Bazzill, WorldWin); patterned paper (Creative Imaginations); rub-on letters (American Crafts); Misc: Century Gothic font

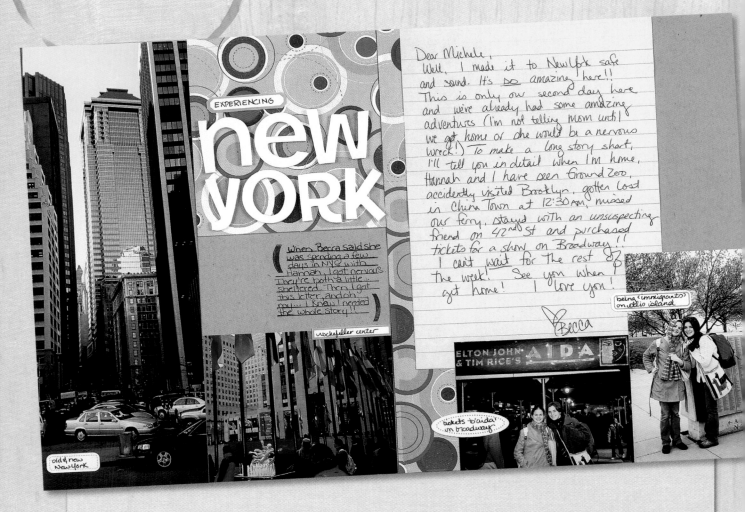

Do you save every letter you receive? I assume that because you scrapbook, you probably do. Use those letters on your pages! Let them tell the story, or better yet, write your own response to the letter. My sister traveled to New York City with our cousin while they were in college. When I got the letter telling what they had experienced, I was so worried and yet so excited for them. Preserving those emotions on a page will remind me years down the road what it was like to be young and adventurous!

Supplies: Cardstock (Bazzill); patterned paper (Cloud 9); letter stickers (American Crafts, Scenic Route); journaling stamp (Autumn Leaves); pen (Zig); ink (Clearsnap)

Dear Mom and Dad,

Please don't be mad at me. I'm just a curious little boy. I want to know what's going on at all times – even when I'm supposed to be in bed. Remember that night you came down at 10 p.m. and found me asleep under the dining room table with a Pledge cloth in my hand? I was just curious about dusting. And remember that night you guys were talking and the words "Silly Putty" came up, then you jumped a foot when you heard me yell, "That's my Silly Putty!" because you thought I was asleep hours ago? I just wanted to know what you people talk about after I leave the room. I do that a lot. In fact, I've gotten so good at it that I can sneak across the creaky floors, up the squeaky stairs, and lay at the top to listen to you, and you never even know it. It was an accident that I started to fall asleep – it was just so late, and you guys just kept talking and didn't know I was there!

I know you're more relieved that I never fell than you are mad. You know how high and steep those crazy steps are – imagine how scary they are to a three-year-old!

Anyway, thanks for laughing and taking pictures instead of being mad. I'll try to stop.

Love,
Henry

One fun way to use a different voice on your page is to write a letter in the words of someone else. It allows you to view an event through someone else's eyes and see events from a different perspective. When Henry was small, he used to sneak out of bed at night to spy on us. I could have written about it in a factual way, but realized it was much more entertaining to pretend to be a three year old. And even better to use a font that looks like a child actually wrote it!

Supplies: Cardstock (Bazzill); patterned paper (Autumn Leaves, Scenic Route, Sonburn); transparency (Hambly); letter stickers (Doodlebug); clip (Making Memories); embellishments (Artistic Scrapper, Cloud 9, KI Memories); Misc: Another font

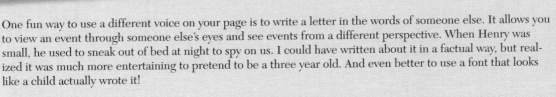

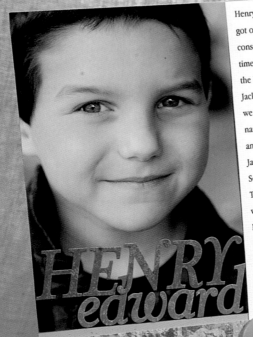

Henry's name was fairly easy. While Marc and I were dating, we somehow got on the topic of kids' names, and we both said we liked "Henry." Weird, considering we didn't generally have the same taste on anything. When the time came and we were about to have a baby, "Henry" was definitely on the list. But so were "Jack" and "Edward."

Jack was nixed fairly quickly because it was getting way too trendy. Also, we knew we liked Edward for a middle name, but "J. Edward" was a family name on my side, and we were trying to avoid family names. And Marc has an uncle named Jack … again, the family name thing. (Turns out, Uncle Jack's middle name is Edward. Huh.)

So we were left with Henry and Edward.

The biggest factor for me, though, was that we took a trip to New England when I was five months pregnant. While there, we spent a day at Walden Pond, wandering around and soaking in the atmosphere and walking in Henry David Thoreau's footsteps. Being in Thoreau's home during our favorite time of year (autumn) and carrying our first child, it occurred to me that this was fate's way of saying, "Come on … you KNOW what you're going to name this child!"

Don't even get me started on how trendy the name Henry is now, though.

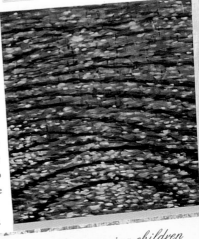

HENRY DAVID THOREAU

Walden and Civil Disobedience

A novel approach to naming children

We tried for nearly two years to have a second child, but it just wasn't working. Finally, I got pregnant. Then I miscarried.

A month later, my grandpa passed away. He was a lawyer, a Congressman, a fighter for civil rights, and an advocate of basic decency. Throughout his career, the media referred to him as an Atticus Finch-type person. Once I read "To Kill a Mockingbird" to figure out what they meant, I was in love with the story.

Five months after my Grandpa died, I found myself pregnant again. And I instantly knew it would be a girl. And I knew that "Harper" made perfect sense … it was a way to remember my Grandpa's legacy, as well as tie in the literary name thing we had going on.

She was supposed to be Harper Eleanor, though, so that her initials and Henry's would be the same. But then Henry went to a sibling preparation class at the hospital, and the baby in the video was named Lily. Henry came home all excited that he was going to have a baby sister named Lily. We tried to explain that her name would be Harper, but Henry wanted none of it. So we agreed to give her the middle name Lillian, so Henry could call her Lily whenever he wanted to. And he did. For a year. Then decided Harper was an okay name, too.

TO KILL A MOCKINGBIRD

The triumphant bestseller that the New York Times calls "The best of the year… exciting… marvelous"

a novel by HARPER LEE

THE PULITZER PRIZE WINNER

INFORM VS. OBSERVE

There are two basic functions of journaling: informing and observing. Writing to share information or an observation may sound like the same thing, but they have totally different purposes.

When journaling as a way to inform, you will generally use the principle of the "five Ws": Who, What, Where, When, and Why (and sometimes How). It's pretty easy to find the five Ws when sharing about holidays and events. However, finding a way to share information in an authentic voice isn't so easy. Written information tends to come out dry and bland, like a news release. It tells what happened, but without much emotion or life, so you have to take care to remember the emotion, or answer the five Ws in a creative, less obvious way.

Unlike informing, observing isn't looking at the big picture and all of its components; it is looking instead at one component through a microscope. Observation still informs a reader—telling how something looks or sounds or makes you feel. But observations are always from your perspective—what *you* see, hear, think, feel. So writing an observation usually results in journaling that has more life and reveals your authentic voice.

Whether you inform or observe is really up to you. Look at your photos or your story and decide what they tell. Just be sure to engage the reader in whatever you do.

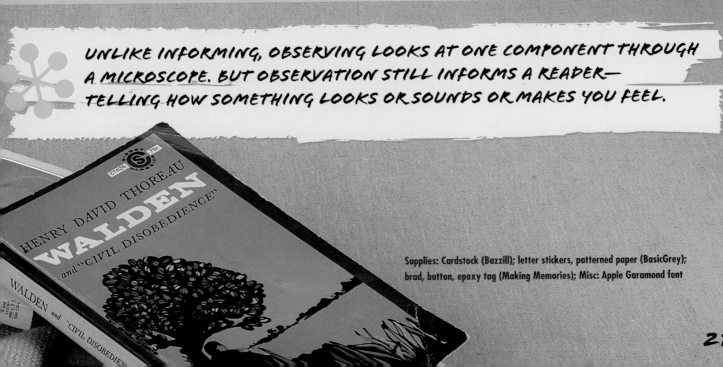

UNLIKE INFORMING, OBSERVING LOOKS AT ONE COMPONENT THROUGH A MICROSCOPE. BUT OBSERVATION STILL INFORMS A READER—TELLING HOW SOMETHING LOOKS OR SOUNDS OR MAKES YOU FEEL.

Supplies: Cardstock (Bazzill); letter stickers, patterned paper (BasicGrey); brad, button, epoxy tag (Making Memories); Misc: Apple Garamond font

Use the five Ws with emotion or in a creative way to reveal your voice along with the information.

Marc and I got engaged on December 23, 1995, and on December 24th he drove down to Indianapolis to be with his family. That evening, it started to snow. It was that quiet, perfect snow that makes you feel like you're inside a snow globe.

It was so perfect that my entire family - parents, sister, grandparents, aunts and uncles and cousins ... all 15 of us - bundled up and headed out. My grandparents lived on a lake at the edge of a college campus, so off we all trudged around the lake, visiting professors and faculty who lived nearby so we could carol them. We returned to the house full of holiday spirit and ready to drink hot cocoa, crack nuts on the hearth, eat Chex mix, and do all of our Christmas Eve traditions. And watch the snow fall.

Christmas morning came, the world was white, and the snow was still falling. We opened gifts, and the snow started to come down harder. It was warm enough that the flakes were fat and sticky and clinging to everything. By lunchtime, snow covered all the trees, and it was falling so hard that we couldn't see across the lake.

My college roommate was at her in-laws' house down the road, and she called to congratulate me on the engagement and invited me over so she could see my ring. I laced up my boots, put on my hat and mittens, and off I went.

The snow was so thick that I could hear it falling; the world was in complete white-out, and the snow was up to my knees. There were no cars and no noise anywhere, except the yells of some kids who were sledding. I was in a sheer state of bliss, but I didn't know if it was from the amazing snow or the diamond on my finger and thought that this time next year I would be married to the love of my life. And I wished so badly that Marc could have been there to share this incredible Christmas snow with me.

The walk was actually tiring because I had to trudge through the deep, heavy snow, but it was perfect. It was like Norman Rockwell and Thomas Kincaid and Currier & Ives all rolled together.

I want a snow like that every single year. And I never want to experience it without Marc again.

Maybe that's why we moved to Minnesota.

The Perfect Snow

This layout is straight-up information. Yet, it's definitely me talking. I adore the snow, especially snow that falls all day long, piles up and covers the world. That is conveyed in the journaling, but it isn't wordy and doesn't try too hard. One way to make sure information comes across in an authentic voice is to put yourself back in the situation and remember how you felt and why, what you smelled, what you saw and heard. If you try to capture the feelings and sensations as you answer the five Ws, your journaling will bring the reader into the moment with you.

Supplies: Cardstock (Bazzill); patterned paper (Chatterbox, Daisy D's, Paper Salon); letter stickers (K&Co.); glitter (JudiKins, Diamond Dust); chalk (Pebbles); Misc: Times New Roman font

Just to prove that informing doesn't have to be a long-winded endeavor, I give you this layout. The "who" is implied . . . it's my daughter, Harper. The "what" is that she learned overnight how to sit up. The "where" is pretty much unnecessary. "When" is the little date stamp. And "why"? Because her development is progressing out of babyhood. There are 13 words on this page, yet you know all you need about Harper learning to sit up. Do you have stories you can boil down to the basics? Remember, there are no bonus points for writing a full page!

Supplies: Cardstock (Bazzill); patterned paper (Making Memories, Sandylion); lace cardstock (KI Memories); letter stickers (BasicGrey); chipboard and rub-on letters (American Crafts); tags (Paper Salon); buttons (Autumn Leaves, KI Memories, Making Memories); glitter chipboard (Doodlebug); stamp (7gypsies); Misc: paint, pen

---

How do you write informational journaling without bogging it down in details and making it boring? Consider writing it as a "Remember when . . ." letter. Sandra took this approach on her page. She manages to hit all the major points—who, what, when, why and even a little how—in one concise paragraph that's neither dry nor boring, but sweet and infused with Sandra's voice.

Supplies: Patterned paper (American Crafts, KI Memories); chipboard accents (Scenic Route); chipboard number (American Crafts)

Artwork by Sandra Stephens

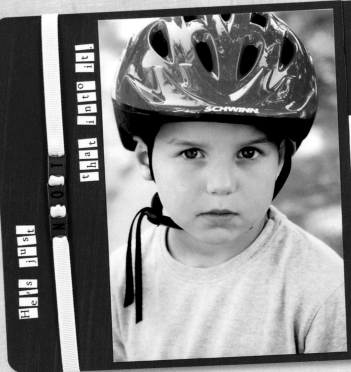

He's just **NOT** that into it.

We thought Henry + bike = good times. But perplexingly, that's not the case. You get on & ride for about ten feet, then you start looking down at the road, back at your wheel, up at the trees. You get off to check out shadows & rocks. You are too distracted to just ride. I do applaud your curiosity though. 8.05

Here's another of my "just the facts" layouts. Not very interesting, right? Wrong! See the look of joy and abandon on Henry's face? See him rocket down the street? No? Well, that's because none of that happened. It's not a typical story about a happy boy on a bike, and that's what makes the information interesting. Sometimes it's not how you write (with an interesting voice) but what you write about (something atypical) that makes informing entertaining. Next time you flip through your pictures and choose some to scrap, see if there is an unexpected story to tell to make your page more engaging.

Supplies: Cardstock (Bazzill); patterned paper (Chatterbox); letter stickers (Making Memories); ribbon (Michaels); Misc: letter slides, pen

tHE StORy behind the photo

Who: Marc, Henry and Harper

What: Posing for a photo

Where: Daley Plaza, Chicago

When: A couple of days before Christmas, 2007

Why: We were spending the day in Chicago as a family while on our way to Indiana for the holidays. It had been weeks of stress, Marc traveling non-stop, and me trying to meet a deadline before Christmas, and we needed a day to just decompress, have some fun, and be a family.

tHE StORy behind the story behind the photo

Who: Marc, Henry and Harper

What: Marc and Henry, laughing in shock, and Harper ducking.

Where: The freezing cold Daley Plaza

When: The Friday before Christmas, 2007

Why: A flock of pigeons took flight right in front of them just as I snapped the photo. Their reaction was priceless, and I'm so thankful I managed to catch it, along with the pigeons . . .

There's no reason you have to answer the five Ws and call it a day. If you look closely at the photo, you'll notice that my family isn't looking at the camera, and there appears to be some bird-shaped blurs. That, my friends, is the real story. I knew the Ws would provide good details for the page, but instead of writing the basic information and leaving it at that, I added "the rest of the story" to give the information zest. Do you have any photographs about which you can find a story behind the story? Share both!

Supplies: Cardstock (Bazzill); letter stickers, patterned paper (Doodlebug); rub-on letters (American Crafts); Misc: Times New Roman font, floss

OBSERVE

Using observation on a layout results in journaling that has life and reveals your authentic voice.

It's easy to journal stories about our kids or family events, but what about all the little things that make up our lives? Observing is a great place to start. Is there a "who" or "what" that triggers a memory? Take Sue's layout. A normal day walking downtown suddenly transported her years back and miles away. You don't need to go into lengthy detail if you don't want to, just try to get out the words to describe how observing something inspires you to remember.

Supplies: Cardstock; chipboard flower and letters (Making Memories); acrylic letters (Heidi Swapp); letter stickers (Creative Imaginations); Misc: 2 Peas Ditzy font, fabric, ink, paint

Artwork by Sue Thomas

What is it about memories? Why are some so elusive while others remain so clear? I mean, I can barely remember where I park my car each day and yet seeing this photo of a sidewalk cafe in downtown Minneapolis takes me back to my Junior year in High School as an exchange student in France. Ahhhh... a cup of hot cocoa (i hadn't developed a taste for coffee yet) and a croissant... the perfect compliments to a morning of people watching from many similar sidewalk cafes in Paris. Merci pour la memoire!

WHY thIS PLacE?

There's just something about the North Shore. Maybe because it's at the same latitude as Maine, a place I love. Maybe because it has pure elemental features – rocks, trees, water – and not much else. Maybe because the dress code is a sweatshirt and hiking boots. Maybe because all I have to do is listen to the waves crash or the rivers rush or the aspens whisper. Maybe because it lacks traffic or Target or cell phone coverage. Maybe because I can breathe freely and deeply and without having to be reminded. Maybe because when I drive up into the Arrowhead and see Lake Superior out the window, I feel as *home* there as I've felt anywhere in my life. Whatever the reason, no matter where I travel in my life and where I may live, the North Shore will always pull me as strongly as a magnetic pole. It is my true North.

The journaling on this page is a series of answers to the question "Why?" in the form of observations about a place. Observations can be about people, places, events or feelings. Come up with your own series of questions and answers that illustrate an observation. You can make an observation, like I did, about why a place affects you the way it does. Or you can ask why something looks the way it does or feels the way it does to develop what you observe. Either way, use your senses to create an accurate picture for your page.

Supplies: Cardstock (Bazzill, WorldWin); letter stickers (KI Memories); die-cut accent, rub-on (Heidi Grace); Misc: Apple Garamond Light font, fiber

"I tend to avoid journaling on holiday scrapbook pages because nothing changes from year to year. I write down names and dates, but that's it. What else can I write?"

Holidays can be tough to journal. But if you really take the time to reflect on your holiday, chances are you'll find a story to write—and a different story to tell next year.

Take this layout. It isn't an obvious Easter layout in that there are no shots of kids in frilly dresses or searching under cushions for eggs. But I found a story in the holiday—about how Easter has become the default holiday for getting together with my family—and that's my journaling. Now, would I journal about that every year? Obviously not. Next year, I'll find something new to write about: Maybe all the eggs will break, or we'll get a huge snowstorm. Or I'll just write about how pretty all the eggs are, and reminisce about Easter as a kid.

Another holiday idea is to write lists of every present your family received that year for Christmas or Hanukkah or birthdays. Over the years, you can then look back and remember all the fun or silly or strange gifts you've gotten, and that in itself might trigger some great journaling!

Attn:

Easter will be held in Minnesota

Thank you

happy easter

Remember

For whatever reason, Easter seems to have become the default holiday during which my family treks to Minnesota for a visit. Surely it isn't because of the weather ... Minnesota is still cold in March/April, and the possibility of a new foot of snow isn't yet out of the question. And it isn't because of some long-standing tradition of church and ham and pretty dresses. All we do for Easter is color a bowlful of eggs and then track them down the following morning. And eat chocolate. Lots of chocolate. It's a given three-day-weekend, so maybe that's why. But whatever the reason, I love it. There are more laughs while coloring eggs, and more eggs to track down. It may be only three days, but I'll take it.

Supplies: Cardstock (Bazzill); patterned paper (Paper Source); die-cut paper (KI Memories); brad, epoxy stickers, letter stickers (Making Memories); paper flowers (Prima); tag (K&Co.); rub-ons (October Afternoon); buttons (SEI, unknown); Misc: Tradition Sans Light font

You and elizabeth found this caterpillar in our garden. we put "her" in the bug box. You fed "her" a lot of milkweed. She got fat made her crysalis. 14 days later...

a BEAUTIFUL butterfly emerged AMAZING!

CHANGE

june 2007

eva, change can lead to some BEAUTIFUL things...embrace change! ♥ mom

Artwork by Catherine Feegel-Erhardt

Catherine used the observation of a caterpillar as a starting point for her journaling about change. She was able to connect a caterpillar's metamorphosis to the encouragement she gives her daughters to welcome change in their lives. Is there anything you observe closely that can become a metaphor? Maybe it's the way a garden grows, or leaves change, or coffee dries in the bottom of a cup. When we look with our hearts as well as our eyes, we can find meaning everywhere in the world around us.

Supplies: Cardstock; patterned paper (A2Z, SEI); butterfly accent, decorative tape, rhinestones, sticker accents (Heidi Swapp); Misc: buttons, ink, paint

Marc and I were talking to Henry the other day, and one of the things we asked was, "What is your favorite thing to do?" Expecting him to answer Legos or video games or playing with friends, we were taken aback when he said, "Reading!"

I have to admit, I'm sort of surprised by how hard the reading bug has gripped him. Henry takes after Marc in so many ways, yet this reading thing ... that's all me! Who knew he would take to it so enthusiastically?

We always knew Henry was "gifted" ... those "Is Your Child Gifted and Talented?" lists always sound exactly like him. So I guess it shouldn't have been a surprise that he's a reader. But it was. One night when Henry was four, we were lying in his bed, reading bedtime stories, and he asked if he could read to us. And he did. He read the first page perfectly. He turned the page and read that one perfectly too. Marc and I just thought, well, we've read this book so many times that he has it memorized. To test our theory, we flipped to a random page in the middle of the book, and by golly if Henry didn't read THAT page perfectly!

When did he learn to read??

Now, at nearly eight, Henry keeps stacks of books in progress on his dresser. And more on the floor. And looks forward to weekly library visits as if they were holidays. He zipped through the Lemony Snicket series, the Magic Tree House books were child's play, he devours books about science and nature and pirates and spies, and he is currently engrossed in "Black Beauty." And "The Adventures of Tom Sawyer" is on deck.

Amazing.

I love that he loves to read. Books will take him anywhere he wants to go in life. And I hope it's a passion that continues to grow in him, if for no other reason than it gives us something in common. Taking him to the library or bookstore is such a fun experience.

Besides, I have a feeling Marc gets everything else.

HE'S A rEADer

When I took these photos of Henry reading on the front steps, surrounded by stacks of books, my observation wasn't so much physical as it was emotional. I recognized myself so much in what he was doing. Everyday observations can trigger a memory or comparison, so paying attention to the things around you can help you find the harder-to-spot topics for your layouts. Make your observation, then take it a step further in your journaling.

Supplies: Cardstock (Bazzill); patterned paper (My Mind's Eye, Scenic Route); letter stickers (Collage Press); border stickers (My Mind's Eye); photo corners (Making Memories); Misc: Apple Garamond Light font, floss

---

How many times do you catch yourself saying, "It's just an observation"? Well, put those observations to good use! What do you observe? And what conclusions do you draw? I find that when the words "just an observation" come out of my mouth, usually it's in response to something that either made me think or amused me. And those are things worth writing on a page. Sometimes your best material is stuff that makes an impression on you … and there's nothing dry or flat about that.

Supplies: Cardstock (Bazzill); patterned paper (Autumn Leaves, Creative Imaginations, Heidi Grace); letter stickers (Colorbök); rub-on letters (Reminisce); Misc: Gautami font

just an Observation

Your side →

The door ←

Marc and I were talking the other day about an article I read on side-of-the-bed sleeping preferences of couples. The majority of those surveyed said they always sleep on a certain side of the bed, whether they sleep at home or a hotel.

I looked at Marc and said, "Do you realize that wherever we sleep and no matter how I arrange the room, you are always on the side furthest from the door?"

He said, "Yeah. I do that on purpose."

My first thought was, *yeah you do.* Then I'm first in line when a kid wakes in the middle of the night or gets up at 6 a.m.

But Marc's reasoning? He's slept furthest from the door since he was a kid, because he wants to have enough reaction time to defend himself in case of attack.

Hmm.

Either way, I think I'm screwed.

GET SOME HELP FROM OTHERS

It's okay to get a little help with your words every now and then. Yes, that's right, I'm giving you permission to base a layout around words that are not your own. But of course, there's a catch: Don't use others' words as the meat of a page; think of them as just the ketchup.

I'll admit it: There are times when my favorite musicians or writers say what's in my heart much better than I can. Sometimes their words perfectly describe what I'm thinking or feeling before I even know what to think or how I feel. It's perfectly fine to get inspiration from songs, books and quotes. That's why those words are written—to inspire us and move us. The trick is to use them as a springboard for your layout, not as your only words. Think about why a song reminds you of a specific moment. Think about why you react strongly to a particular passage. Think about why you sing a certain lullaby to your child. This should be the stuff of your journaling.

I may be a writer but there are times when my family or someone else says something so perfect their words have to be the main words on a layout. Conversations are a great way to inspire your journaling. This may sound a bit obvious, but journaling with a clear authentic voice is easy when you use actual spoken words. Stage a conversation, if you must, but make sure you write it down! When your kids say something precocious or insightful or hilarious, record it for posterity. When your spouse is wrapped up in his all-consuming interest or hobby, ask him about it and then write out the conversation. These nuggets of communication create a charming record of your family's lives and give you the inspiration you need to add words to your page.

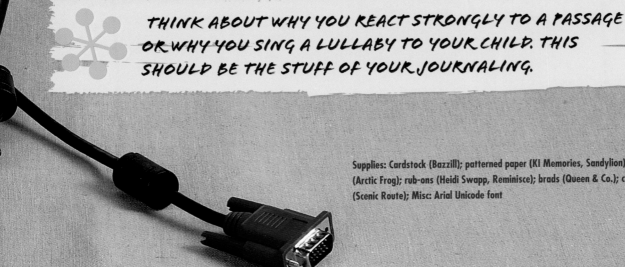

THINK ABOUT WHY YOU REACT STRONGLY TO A PASSAGE OR WHY YOU SING A LULLABY TO YOUR CHILD. THIS SHOULD BE THE STUFF OF YOUR JOURNALING.

Supplies: Cardstock (Bazzill); patterned paper (KI Memories, Sandylion); letter stickers (Arctic Frog); rub-ons (Heidi Swapp, Reminisce); brads (Queen & Co.); chipboard accent (Scenic Route); Misc: Arial Unicode font

LYRICS & QUOTATIONS

When you can't find your own words, use songs, book excerpts and quotations that inspire and move you to provide a springboard for journaling.

She'd tell him about her dreams - he'd just shoot 'em down. Lord, he loved to make her cry. "You're crazy for believin' you'll ever leave the ground," he said... "only angels know how to fly." And with a broken wing, she still sings. She keeps an eye on the sky. With a broken wing, she carries her dreams. Man, you ought to see her fly. One sunday mornin', she didn't go to church. He wondered why she didn't leave. He went up to her bedroom, found a note by the window, with the curtains blowin' in the breeze, and with a broken wing, she still sings. She keeps an eye on the sky. With a broken wing, she carries her dreams. Man, you ought to see her fly. With a broken wing, she carries her dreams. Man, you ought to see her fly.

~ Martina McBride

with a broken wing

It seems like an ordinary photograph. A casual family portrait. In reality, it's the last photo that we ever had taken as a family unit. It was taken in the midst of sadness & anger & the realization that a marriage was over. It was taken of a girl who was trying to hard to hang on...trying so hard to do what was right for herself & her little girl. The lyrics of a Broken Wing still bring a sense of strength...they remind me that, no matter what, this girl can fly....

Artwork by Katrina Simeck

Many times, there is that one song that speaks above all others because you feel it was written just for you. Katrina has a connection like that to Martina McBride's song, "With a Broken Wing." In her journaling she doesn't go into detail about why the song is so meaningful for her. What she does do is write about how the lyrics come to mind when she looks at this particular photograph, and how one line of the song—"you ought to see her fly"—became her mantra. Find the song that is your anthem, and write about how it moves you.

Supplies: Cardstock (WorldWin); patterned paper (BasicGrey, Making Memories, October Road); rub-on letters (American Crafts); brads (Stemma); flowers (Making Memories); lace (Melissa Frances); digital paper by Gina Cabrera (Digital Design Essentials); digital photo frame by Katie Pertiet (Designer Digitals); digital wing accents (Paper Moons)

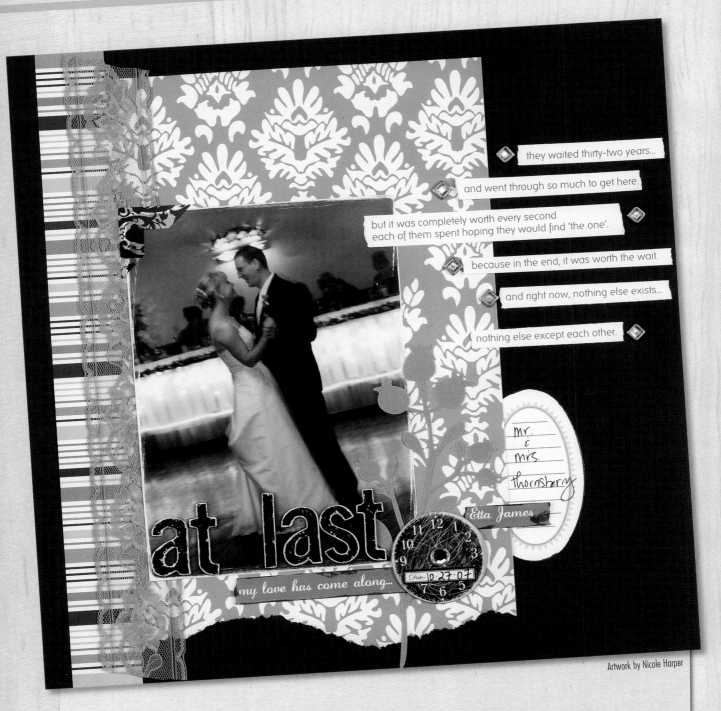

they waited thirty-two years...

and went through so much to get here.

but it was completely worth every second each of them spent hoping they would find 'the one'.

because in the end, it was worth the wait.

and right now, nothing else exists...

nothing else except each other.

mr. & mrs. Thornsberry

Etta James

at last

my love has come along...

Artwork by Nicole Harper

Even if words don't have any special meaning to you personally, they might fit a page about someone else perfectly. As Nicole's journaling on this layout reveals, her brother and new sister-in-law spent a lot of time looking for the right person, and, as the song says, at last love did come along for them. Find words that perfectly describe what you are trying to say with your page, then include them as a title or embellishment. They will add just the right touch of poignancy and clarity to your own words.

Supplies: Cardstock; patterned paper (American Crafts); chipboard letters (BasicGrey); transparency (Hambly); journaling tag (Scenic Route); brads, paint (Making Memories); sticker accent (7gypsies, EK Success); chipboard clock (Heidi Swapp); rhinestone (Darice); Misc: glitter, vintage lace

PROBLEM SOLVED

"I know that I need to put more meaning into what I write, but the importance of the words is daunting. How do I overcome my fear of not doing my stories justice?"

If I can give one piece of advice, it's this: Don't stress about getting it right! Getting any writing at all on a page is half the battle. Once you are in the routine of thinking about the emotion a page elicits or a memory you want to capture and then writing it down, you can move on to finessing how "meaningful" it sounds.

Start small, and work up to full-on openness. My journaling on the page "History Repeating" is an example of starting small. When I realized how eerily similar were these photos of me and my daughter at roughly the same age, a million thoughts popped into my head. But instead of bogging down the page with words and risk meandering pointlessly, I chose to highlight a few of my initial thoughts. I can always go back to these thoughts and flesh them out one by one on subsequent pages, but for this page, simple is good enough.

When you start with the basics, it gives you the springboard to dive into deeper stuff later when you are ready. The fact that you write anything at all will do more justice to your stories than leaving them off your pages altogether.

HISTORY repeating

2007   1976

While visiting my parents this summer, my mom surprised me by pulling out a little outfit I had worn when I was Harper's age. It fit Harp almost perfectly. I remembered the photo of me wearing the outfit and took Harper outside to find a tree so we could take a similar photo. Amazingly, Harper leaned up against the tree in almost an identical pose to the one I had done 30 years before.

We laughed at the sense of déjà vu we felt about the Harper in the outfit with the tree. But now that I look at the photos, I wonder in what other ways her life will mirror mine.

Will she suffer the same insecurities and teasing and isolation and depression? Will she be strengthened or weakened by the challenges in her life? Will she keep the pure joy and delight in life that she has right now? Will her crazy sense of humor grow as she does? Will she be smart and driven? Will she be successful in her choices? Will she meet and marry the love of her life? Will she reach her 30s and realize that everything she went through up to that point was all in the past, and the future holds more happiness than she could possibly imagine?

I don't want history to repeat itself with my girl. I want her to make her own path and her own choices and mistakes. As long as she's happy and safe, she has my blessing to find her own way.

Supplies: Cardstock (Bazzill); patterned paper (BasicGrey, My Mind's Eye); chipboard letters and accent (Creative Imaginations); Misc: Apple Garamond and Gigi fonts, ink

happy ever after

The morning sunrise spread her wings, while the moon hung in the sky. Held the sea in your hands, and happy ever after in your eyes.

Every star in the night promises the dawn. I will be there if you fall, to ever so heavily rest upon. All that I can give you is forever yours

to keep. Wake up every day with a dream, and happy ever after in your eyes. – Ben Harper

I first heard "Happy Ever After" on the way to shoot Dave and Jessica's wedding, and I fell instantly in love. I played it on repeat during the 30 minute drive to their house, the 45 minute drive to the Arboretum for the wedding, and the 45 minute drive back to my house.

I now have a Pavlovian response to the song. Whenever I hear it, that day is suddenly all around me. But hearing it and subsequently thinking of Dave and Jess then also makes me think of Marc, as all things happy, fallish, and weddingy inevitably do. And the lyrics, specifically, make me think of my wonderful life with my amazing husband. It hasn't always been (and won't always be) perfect or easy, but I truly do see *happy ever after* when I look at him.

Had this song been around in 1996, it absolutely would have been in our wedding. And I'm so happy that it will always remind me of Dave and Jess's big day. Two perfect memories ... one perfect song.

When I heard the song "Happy Ever After" last fall while driving to photograph the wedding of some friends, the song really spoke to me. The more I hit the repeat button and listened to the words, the more it made me think of my husband and our own wedding day. This scrapbook page brings together the two different weddings, two different couples, two different reasons why the song is so meaningful to me. Is there a song that speaks to you in that way? Share it on a page!

Supplies: Cardstock (Bazzill); patterned paper (Paper Source); letter stickers (BasicGrey); chipboard accents (Heidi Grace); Misc: Ancient Script and Californian fonts, ink

happiness is having a large, loving, caring, close-knit family

... in another city.

I LOVE MY FAMILY; I REALLY DO. BUT THE FUNNY THIS IS THAT I THINK WE ALL LOVE EACH OTHER A LITTLE MORE NOW THAT MARC AND I LIVE 600 MILES AWAY. IS THAT CRAZY? THERE WERE ALWAYS CONFLICTS OR GUILT TRIPS OR FEELINGS BEING HURT WHEN I LIVED AT HOME AND IN MY HOMETOWN, BUT AS SOON AS I GOT MARRIED AND MOVED THREE STATES AWAY, THINGS IMPROVED DRAMATICALLY. MAYBE GEORGE BURNS WAS RIGHT ... MAYBE HAPPINESS TRULY IS LIVING CITIES APART FROM YOUR FAMILY. IT SEEMS TO HAVE WORKED FOR US.

together
family
laugh

Hi, I'm Michele, and I'm a quote-a-holic. I keep notebooks full of quotations that inspire me. You never know when you'll need the perfect words, right? This quote immediately made me think of my family when I first heard it. Naturally, it had to become the basis of a page. But instead of using only the quote, it became the title, and my journaling expands on the quote's meaning. On your own pages, use quotes as the catalyst for making you think more deeply about a subject. Then write about what you discovered from those words.

Supplies: Cardstock (Bazzill); patterned paper (Autumn Leaves, Hambly, Scenic Route); transparency (Hambly); word stickers (Making Memories); sticker accents (EK Success); brads, die-cut tag (K&Co.); rub-ons (October Afternoon); Misc: Sandy Text and Wallow fonts

when I told him
I had a major in
ENGLISH
He said *too bad for you,*
this is america,
& he started me out at the bottom.

- brian andreas

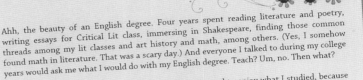

Ahh, the beauty of an English degree. Four years spent reading literature and poetry, writing essays for Critical Lit class, immersing in Shakespeare, finding those common threads among my lit classes and art history and math, among others. (Yes, I somehow found math in literature. That was a scary day.) And everyone I talked to during my college years would ask me what I would do with my English degree. Teach? Um, no. Then what?

Well ... that was actually a good question. I knew I wanted to enjoy what I studied, because by default I should then like whatever job I would find that used my degree. And I love to read, so an English major it would be. And I love to write, so I had an emphasis in print media ... didn't figure that one out until late in the game, and there was no way I was staying an extra semester just to have a full minor. Who cares about minors anyway??

I dabbled with the idea of Public Relations after working as the PR Director's student assistant all through college. Then I got a job at a newspaper and thought, "Alright. I'll work for a newspaper." But that lasted only until Marc got transferred to Minneapolis three months after our wedding.

Once we got to Minnesota, I had to really figure out my plan. I tried advertising, and was hired to be an administrative assistant. And even though I was told that writing work would find its way onto my desk, they ended up hiring a copywriter. (Wait ... no one told me they were looking for a *writer!!*) Oh, but I *did* get to wash out their coffee mugs in the bathroom and change light bulbs.

I then moved onto magazine publishing, but all that came of that was assuming deniability about the publisher's practice of double billing clients and refusing certified mail that contained litigation papers.

That job left me *thisclose* to a nervous breakdown, so I landed at Pottery Barn for six months. Then a friend contacted me about an editorial position at a children's curriculum book publishing house. It sounded like heaven! I interviewed, got the job, and immediately found out I was pregnant with Henry. So much for that.

When I was in college and spent my days reading beautiful words, of course I had visions of my life with an English degree: a small, sunny studio apartment in a major city, a typewriter, stacks of notebooks and mugs full of pens, a cat curled up on a pillow while I wrote my days away. Or maybe I left that apartment each morning in funky outfits to go work for some major publishing house, where I would read manuscripts all day long and would find that one perfect one that would win the next major literary accolade.

Those visions never included washing mugs or leaving work under the unfailing stare of a dictator boss who monitored our every move from his conference room office (because it had the most windows).

I'm not sure there is a good answer for "What will you do with your English degree?" unless you know you want to teach. English. But one thing I have learned over the years is that an English degree can open the world in so many, many ways. Even if it is only to fetch light bulbs for awhile.

she said

Brian Andreas is one of my favorite artists, and his poetry always inspires me. His piece on being an English major is one of my favorites, so I used the poem not only as inspiration for this page, but also as its title. The journaling, though, is my own thoughts on life with a degree in English lit. Quotations can inspire your pages, but don't feel like you have to journal about them. Write whatever thoughts rise to the surface when you think about the words. Heck, you don't even have to use the quote on the page . . . just use it as a springboard for the layout.

Supplies: Cardstock (Bazzill); label holder, patterned paper, rub-ons (Heidi Grace); chipboard accent (Scenic Route); brads (American Crafts); Misc: 2 Peas Favorite Things, Agent Orange, Chaparral Pro and Desert Dogs fonts

CONVERSATIONS

Conversations are great for jumpstarting your journaling, and using spoken words is an easy way to ensure an authentic voice.

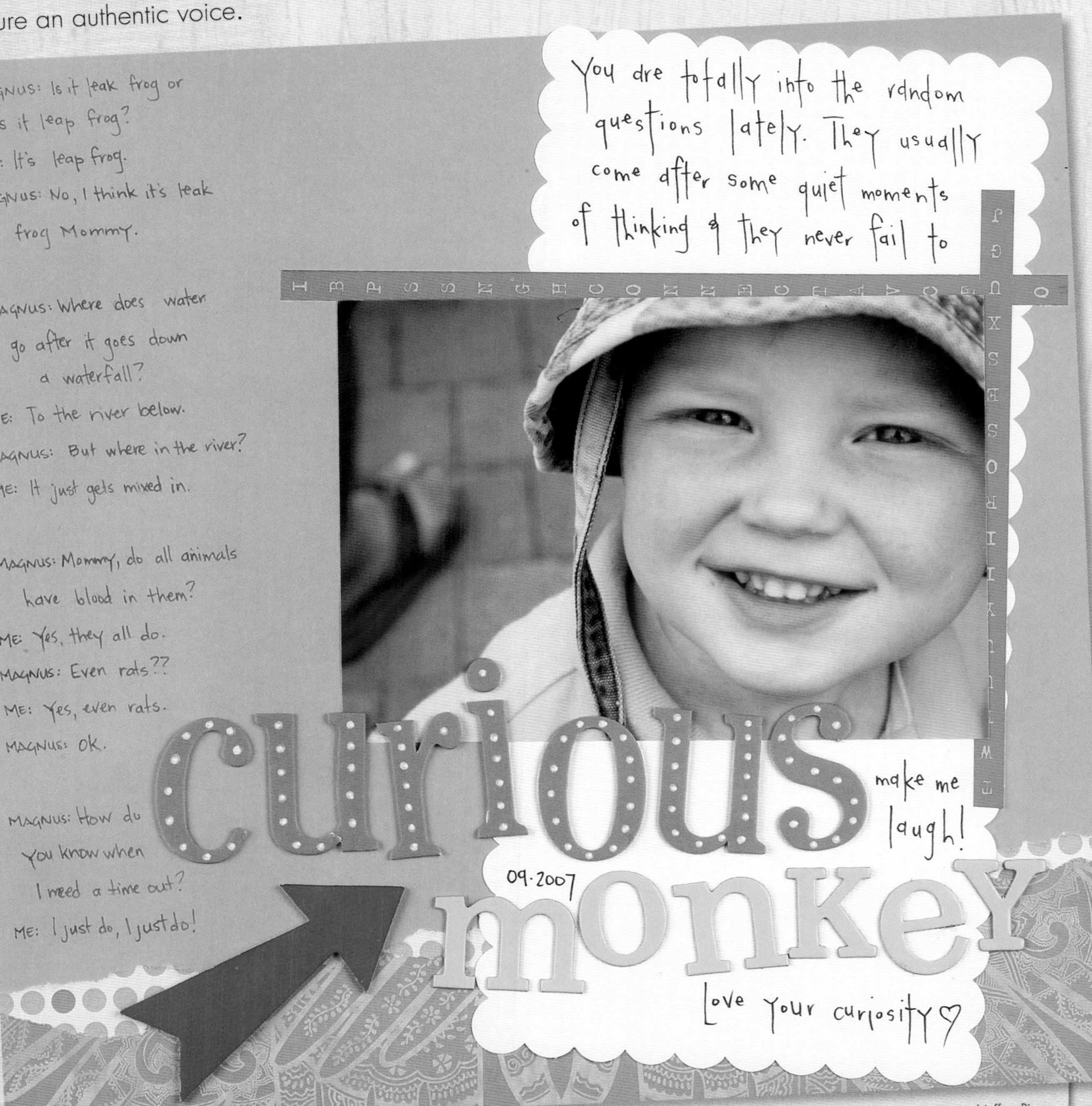

MAGNUS: Is it leak frog or is it leap frog?

ME: It's leap frog.

MAGNUS: No, I think it's leak frog Mommy.

MAGNUS: Where does water go after it goes down a waterfall?

ME: To the river below.

MAGNUS: But where in the river?

ME: It just gets mixed in.

MAGNUS: Mommy, do all animals have blood in them?

ME: Yes, they all do.

MAGNUS: Even rats??

ME: Yes, even rats.

MAGNUS: OK.

MAGNUS: How do you know when I need a time out?

ME: I just do, I just do!

You are totally into the random questions lately. They usually come after some quiet moments of thinking & they never fail to

curious make me laugh!

09·2007 monkey

love your curiosity♡

Artwork by Crystal Jeffrey Rieger

Who needs to come up with something to write when kids provide the perfect journaling every time they open their mouths? You can create a page around one specific statement or conversation, or you can group together several quotes and let your own journaling tie them all together. For this layout, Crystal pulled together a few of her son's more thoughtful questions to show that he's always wondering about things. Gather quotes from a child that are related in some way, and use them as a way to illustrate that child's personality.

Supplies: Cardstock; patterned paper (Dove of the East, Karen Foster, KI Memories); chipboard letters (Heidi Swapp, K&Co.); chipboard arrow (Deluxe Designs); paint (Delta); Misc: pen

{just} i noticed

Photograph No. 517

MONDAY		TUESDAY
you've been giving me tons of hugs lately.... i not

| WEDNESDAY | | THURSDAY |
that i'm complaining, but i asked why... your answer? ? "Well...," won't be able to

| FRIDAY | |
give you any while i'm @

| SATURDAY | | SUNDAY |
school... so i thought you might like to save 'em up." (& you were absolutely right.) ♥

'AUG 2 7 2007

'2|7 | '2|8 (a)

Artwork by Nicole Harper

Sometimes an offhand remark sparks a thought that's worth writing down. That's just what Nicole did when her daughter told her why she was giving her so many hugs lately. Has someone ever said something to you that was so unexpected it drew out an emotional response? Write it down, and keep it forever. Nicole knows there will probably come a time when her daughter won't hug her every day, so making note of her thoughtfulness at eight years old is something worth journaling.

Supplies: Cardstock; patterned paper (Anna Griffin, Scenic Route); transparency (Hambly); letter stickers (American Crafts, Making Memories); chipboard accent (Scenic Route); journaling tags (Heidi Swapp); stamp (Purple Onion); sticker accent (EK Success); Misc: ink, paint, thread, vintage stars and tape measure

M: What do you want to be when you grow up?

H: You know!   M: Was it a robot builder or a video game maker?

H: Robot builder. Well, both. See, I'm gonna build the robots, then have a store. I'll put up a "help wanted" sign, and when I get enough people working in the store to sell the robots, then I can leave to go make video games.

M: Well, then it's a good thing you love math and science, because you'll need that to build the robots AND make the video games. And it's good that you like to read and write because you'll have to write the story for the game.

H: Yeah. And I'll have to know technology, too.

M: Yes, you will.

H: And how to surf the web.

That goes without saying, H. What a kid.

Henry

big plans

This conversation occurred on a ride home from Henry's science enrichment program. He was going on and on about science and what cool projects they'd done, and I mentioned he would make a great scientist when he grew up. He said "nah," so I asked, "What do you want to be when you grow up?" That led to this page. Conversations with children are so precious and worth recording! Not raising a talker? Use a child's artwork as a conversation starter. Then use their artwork to decorate a page. Scans of Henry's drawings illustrate this page better than any store-bought embellishment could.

Supplies: Cardstock (Bazzill); patterned paper (Adornit, Sassafras Lass); transparency (Hambly); chipboard letters (BasicGrey); letter stickers, sticker accents (Heidi Grace); Century Gothic and Typo Slab Serif fonts

Conversation w/ Henry 3.08.0?

Henry: Mommy, did you know I have two sharp pointed upside-down triangle teeth on the top and the bottom of my mouth?

Mommy: Yes. Those are called *canine* teeth. *(Explains "canine," using the word "purpose" to describe why we have different teeth.)*

H: What is "purpose"?

M: *(Defines "purpose")*

H: Then, what's the purpose of the trees?

M: To make oxygen for us to breathe and to clean the air.

H: What's the purpose of grass?

M: To hold the dirt together.

H: What's the purpose of sidewalks?

M: For people to walk on so they don't get hit by buses and cars.

H: What's the purpose of streets?

M: *(Starting to grumble a little)* For the cars to drive on so people can get where they want to go.

H: What's the purpose of signs?

M: To give people information.

H: What's the purpose of me?

M: *(Huh. Now we have an interesting question.)* To be my son. To be smart and kind and loving and obedient so that when you are older, you can do great things in the world.

H: Does everyone have a purpose?

M: Yes. My purpose was to be your mom and to love you and teach you how to be good and kind and smart so that you can be important to the future.

H: What is Daddy's purpose?

M: To be your daddy and to fix computer stuff for many different businesses so they can make money and then our city can make money, which helps our world make money.

H: Oh. I think that's enough purposes for now.

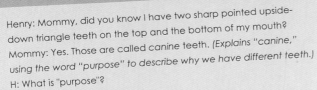

define:

PURPOSE

DATE 11·05

Repeated conversations stick in our heads, and are also a fun way to get some real journaling on a page! Does your child ask you "Why?" a hundred times a day? Do you and your partner always have the same disagreement? Did your parents repeat the same rules every time you walked out the door? This layout was a conversation I had with Henry. Every time he asked me what something's purpose was, I really had to stop and think about it. Sure, repeated words can get, well, repetitive, but they can also inspire some creative thought.

Supplies: Cardstock (Bazzill); patterned paper (Sonburn); chipboard letters (American Crafts); label sticker (EK Success); felt (Fancy Pants); pin (Heidi Grace); tag sticker (7gypsies); ribbon (May Arts, Strano); Misc: Century Gothic font

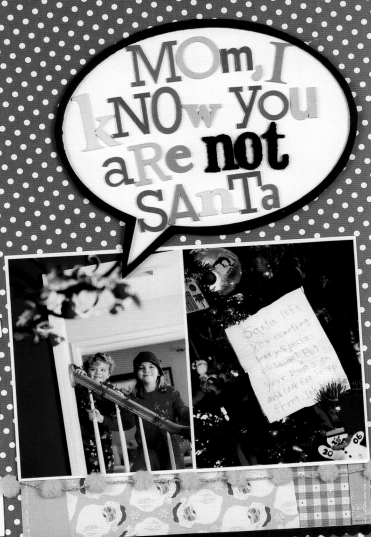

MOm, I kNOw YOu aRe not SAnTa

"Oh?", I replied as I felt my hands begin to sweat.

"Santa's handwriting is different than yours", she stated matter-of-factly.

"You're absolutely right!", I answered. Whew, that was a close one!

I'm so happy Santa has difficulty writing with his left hand. He goes to great lengths to keep the magic alive and I'm sure it's stressful at times.

The different wrapping papers, telling Tiffil Star (the silly elf) what to do every night, sneaking around the house in the dark, and the toughest job of all: finding out about the must-have stocking stuffers. A picture of Comet? Umm…no problem!

Artwork by Sandra Stephens

Every parent dreads the day their child poses a Big Question, but it can also be a time when that child's perspective surprises us. These can be wonderful moments to record and keep. Write out the conversation, then either expand upon what your own observations and feelings are on the subject or what your response is. Either way, those Big Questions can lead to great authentic writing.

Supplies: Cardstock; patterned paper (K&Co.); letter stickers (American Crafts); chipboard letters (Making Memories); chipboard bubble (BamPop); scalloped sticker trim (KI Memories); Misc: Catriel font, ink, paint, ribbon

I look at the mess on my desktop.

I look at the mess of toys on the floor.

I look at the clock and know I should go to bed.

I look at my husband, sitting on the sofa watching the military channel, and think that maybe I should go snuggle with him instead.

I look at the calendar and see the chaos about to ensue.

I look at my life and wonder how I can possibly let go of anything.

But I have to.

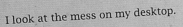

Because without scrapping, all the other stuff becomes a grind.

I need these few hours a week to remind myself that I have a need to create, a need to tell a story, a need to focus on my own thoughts for awhile.

I need these projects to remind myself that I am more than a housewife and stay-home mommy and chauffer and cook and janitor.

I need to know that despite it all, I'm still me.

And I need time, too.

JUST DO IT

For many people, the simple amount of time journaling requires is all it takes to deter them from ever attempting to write. It even deters them from starting a page. Like I asked at the beginning of the book, how many pages do you have with a pre-planned space for journaling that is still blank? Why? Is it a fear of writing the wrong thing? Is it a fear of how you will sound? It is the inconvenience of having to type up and print the journaling?

It is so easy to forget how important the journaling is and just let it slide. But when you look back at pages that have sat wordless for so long, you probably don't even remember all the details of the photos you've documented. This is why writing down thoughts and recording events on layouts is so important. We think we'll always remember, but the truth is that memories slip away faster than we'd like to admit. And remember, you can't write your memories if you don't have a place to put them! Whether you carry a notebook in your purse to record things, or you stretch yourself to create layouts on topics you don't normally scrap, remember that it is important to just do it! You know what stories and memories move you; now let them move you to the scrapping table.

Please stop fretting! I'll show you a few quick, no-stress ways to get journaling down on paper so you'll have it handy when you are ready to sit and scrap. You'll have to motivate yourself to actually record the moment on a layout, but you'll thank me later when you're no longer left to compose a page struggling to remember what you wanted to say.

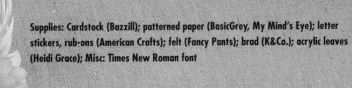

WHETHER YOU CARRY A NOTEBOOK IN YOUR PURSE OR STRETCH YOURSELF TO CREATE LAYOUTS ON TOPICS YOU DON'T NORMALLY SCRAP, REMEMBER THAT IT IS IMPORTANT TO JUST DO IT!

Supplies: Cardstock (Bazzill); patterned paper (BasicGrey, My Mind's Eye); letter stickers, rub-ons (American Crafts); felt (Fancy Pants); brad (K&Co.); acrylic leaves (Heidi Grace); Misc: Times New Roman font

JUST GET IT WRITTEN

Writing down thoughts is so important; it's so easy to forget the details about photos. Remember that details and memories can easily be lost if they aren't written down right away.

SHE WOKE UP WHEN?!

4:50.

That would be *a.m.*

She couldn't find her plugs.

Then 5:11.

Also *a.m.*

Because she needed Chapstick.

Then 5:26.

Yes, still *a.m.*

Because her sheets hurt her back and she needed raspberry torte medicine. (Don't ask.)

And then at 5:48.

a.friggin.m.

I didn't let her give me a reason; just shoved her back in bed.

But she was still up for the day at 6:11.

a.m.

And did I mention she didn't take a nap yesterday?

Apparently now she doesn't eat *OR* sleep.

Lovely.

WHAT'S IT LIKE TO BE YOU?

bundle of joy

You

I NEVER MET A
SLEEPING BABY
I DIDN'T LIKE

UNBELIEVABLE

can you give me some advance warning next time so I can get more than four hours of sleep?!

Stop, drop and write. Literally. When inspiration hits you, stop what you're doing, drop everything and write it down. This layout is a result of this technique. My daughter has been the most noneating, nonsleeping child I've ever known. On this day, she decided that 4:50 a.m. was as good a time as any to start the day. Instead of crumpling into a ball of tears, I decided to take a photo and write the words that popped into my head. The resulting thoughts came out more authentic than if I'd tried to write it much later . . . or after getting some sleep.

Supplies: Cardstock (Bazzill); patterned paper (Making Memories, Scenic Route); letter stickers (BasicGrey); border sticker (My Mind's Eye); sticker accents (7gypsies, BoBunny, Paper Loft, Scenic Route); Misc: Lucida Bright font

I don't know **what** was **more** inspiring ... the **amazing** beauty of split rock lighthouse and gooseberry falls, or the fact that **henry**, at age four, totally kept up with us, mile for mile.

peaceful

majestic

You have a ton of related photos and you're ready to creatively maneuver all those photos across several album pages, and then add embellishments and journaling . . . bah! You'll be scrapping them for a month. Or maybe not. Try wallpapering cardstock with photos and leaving just enough room for a quick journaling block. This is a quick way to use a lot of photos, write down a few thoughts about them, and call it a day. Skip the whole album. Just write.

Supplies: Cardstock (Bazzill); patterned paper (BasicGrey, Creative Imaginations); letter stickers (American Crafts); word stickers (Cloud 9); embroidered accent (Autumn Leaves)

Sometimes you just don't have the time to create layouts. Am I right? This is where $2 photo albums come in handy. Throw in a handful of photos—by topic, event, a year-in-review—and insert the occasional piece of cardstock or index card for quick journaling. When you are ready to scrap, your photos and journaling are right there ready for you. And if you're still out of time later, you could also use lovely notebook-style patterned paper for your journaling, add a few embellishments on the cover and be done with it.

Supplies: Patterned paper (Adornit, Autumn Leaves, Creative Imaginations); letter stickers (Making Memories, Scenic Route); letter stamps (Paper Studio); lined stamp (KI Memories); flowers (Prima); pocket (Making Memories); Misc: buttons, ink, paint, pen, photo album

quick facts

purchased 4625 Portland Ave South in Minneapolis in July '98 for $105,000. Sold it in July '04 for $240,000 .... after 48 hours on the market. I loved this house; Marc, not so much. But it held many great memories.

FiRsT *home*

they **INSPIRE** me

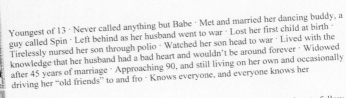

Youngest of 13 · Never called anything but Babe · Met and married her dancing buddy, a guy called Spin · Left behind as her husband went to war · Lost her first child at birth · Tirelessly nursed her son through polio · Watched her son head to war · Lived with the knowledge that her husband had a bad heart and wouldn't be around forever · Widowed after 45 years of marriage · Approaching 90, and still living on her own and occasionally driving her "old friends" to and fro · Knows everyone, and everyone knows her

Married her high school sweetheart · Left small-town Indiana for the first time to follow her husband to Brooklyn, and lived there on her own while he went to war · Widowed before she was 40 · Raised three kids on her own · Watched her son head to war · Loves living on her own in the middle of nowhere · Still gardens to grown her own vegetables every year · Cans and freezes her vegetables for the winter (best.green.beans.ever.) · Keeps perfect files of every gift ever given, in case there's ever a question · Gives all she can, asks for nothing

Married her college sweetheart · Finished school while her husband was fighting in the war · Had four kids · Left behind when her husband went back to war · Left behind as her husband went to work in Washington, DC · Watched her son head to war · Mothered fearlessly and unsentimentally and creatively · Has two patents for teaching aides she developed · Personifies utmost faith and moral character · Would sled, climb trees, and attempt whatever she wanted with the grandkids

to be **STRONG**

Many of us fear we won't get to hear our family's stories, and one day it will be too late. My grandmothers live far away, and I don't get to spend nearly enough time with them. I'm so inspired by what they've lived through and don't want to forget those things. But instead of waiting until I know all their stories, I created this page that lists details about each one, details that inspire me daily to keep on persevering and pushing on. Use what you've got, and don't wait too long.

Supplies: Cardstock (Bazzill); patterned paper (Daisy D's, K&Co., Sassafras Lass); letter stickers (BasicGrey); chipboard letters (Heidi Swapp); rub-ons (K&Co.); Misc: Times New Roman font

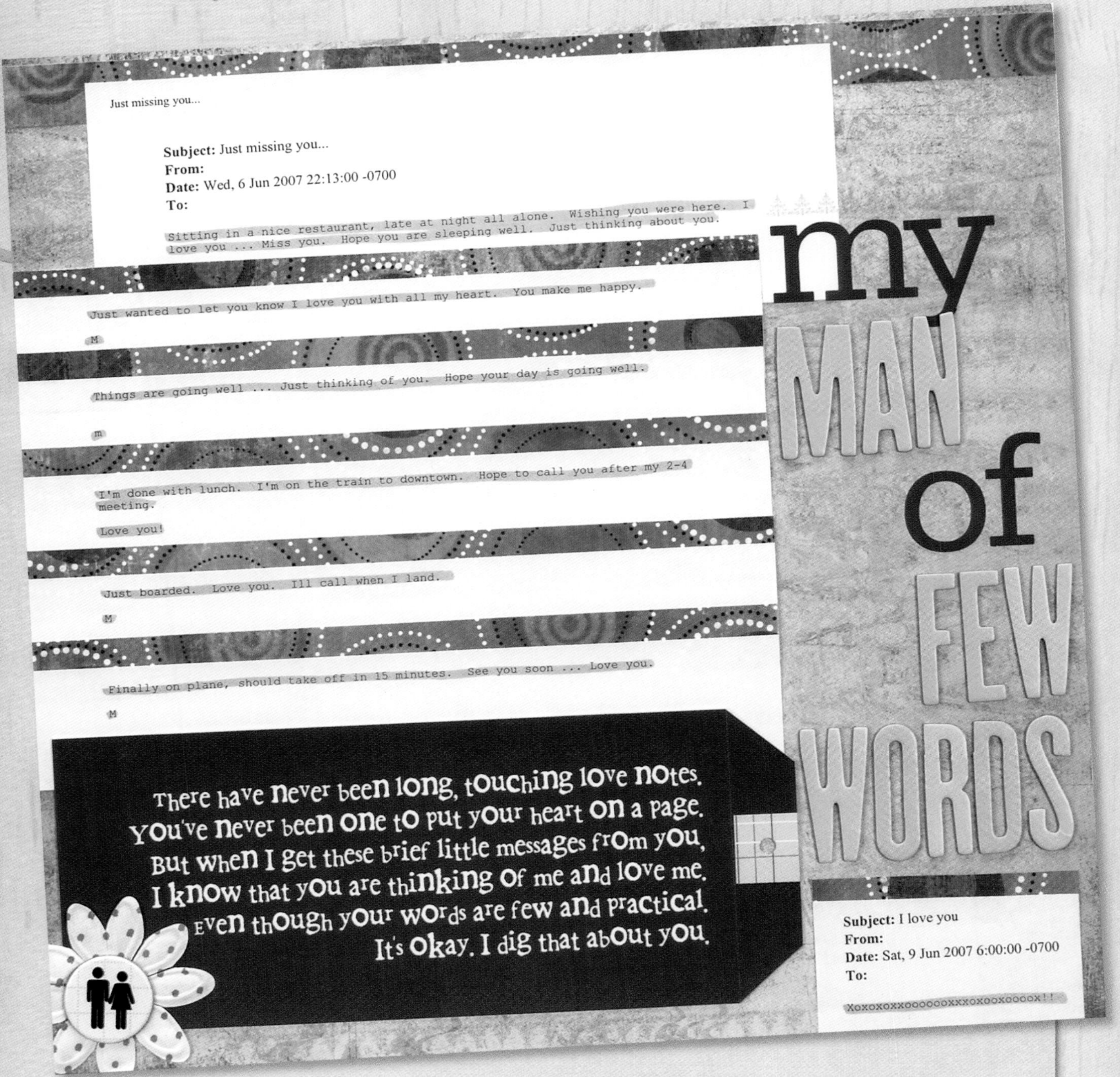

Just missing you...

Subject: Just missing you...
From:
Date: Wed, 6 Jun 2007 22:13:00 -0700
To:

Sitting in a nice restaurant, late at night all alone. Wishing you were here. I love you ... Miss you. Hope you are sleeping well. Just thinking about you.

Just wanted to let you know I love you with all my heart. You make me happy.

M

Things are going well ... Just thinking of you. Hope your day is going well.

m

I'm done with lunch. I'm on the train to downtown. Hope to call you after my 2-4 meeting.

Love you!

Just boarded. Love you. I'll call when I land.

M

Finally on plane, should take off in 15 minutes. See you soon ... Love you.

M

There have never been long, touching love notes.
You've never been one to put your heart on a page.
But when I get these brief little messages from you,
I know that you are thinking of me and love me.
Even though your words are few and practical.
It's okay. I dig that about you.

my MAN of FEW WORDS

Subject: I love you
From:
Date: Sat, 9 Jun 2007 6:00:00 -0700
To:

Xoxoxoxxooooooxxxoxooxooooox!!

This layout was borne of the realization that every e-mail I get from Marc sounds essentially the same. I wanted to document these e-mails, and while doing so, it occured to me that this is a really handy way to get some words on a page. I didn't have to find any photos, and it didn't require a lot of writing on my part. The most time-consuming part was printing out all the e-mails! Using memorabilia is a great way to include words and personality without taking a lot of time. A few quick thoughts on the gathered stuff makes the story your own.

Supplies: Cardstock (Bazzill); patterned paper (BasicGrey, Fancy Pants, Piggy Tales); chipboard letters, letter stickers, rub-on (American Crafts); chipboard accent (Scenic Route); flower (Prima); Misc: 2 Peas Jack Frost font

JUST GET IT ON A LAYOUT

There are so many stories waiting to be told. Just get them scrapped and you'll never have to worry about forgetting the details.

{timeline}

March 10, 2005: Dr Maletta says Baby is big, and I will be induced on Tuesday, March 15. That doesn't work for me; I declare I will get Baby out myself to avoid having my membranes stripped.

March 13: Walk around Bachman's-Marshall Fields Garden Show for two hours with Mom.

March 14: Do several hours of errands and shopping and more walking.

March 14, 3:30 p.m.: Nap; still fighting week-long illness.

5:00 p.m.: Wake up to discover dampness in my pants. Trip to the bathroom confirms water has broken. Mild contractions are noticeable about every seven minutes. Assume I have plenty of time to eat and pack since previous labor and delivery took 21 hours from point of water breaking.

6:30 p.m.: Contractions harder and more frequent now – every three- to five minutes apart. Call doctor and am told to go to the hospital. Guess Marc and I should pack our bags now.

8:00 p.m.: Arrive at Fairview Southdale. Park car and start walking through skyway that crosses six lanes of France Ave. Have to stop five times to let contractions pass.

8:30p.m.: Checked into triage and declared "in labor." Told to walk for an hour, since I am currently only 2cm dilated. This is not a surprise … it took 17 hours to reach 3cm during previous labor. We make it about 30 minutes but contractions are so hard that I can no longer walk. Back to the room, get hooked up to saline and penicillin (because strep test wasn't done yet), and am told I am at 3cm.

9:30-10:30 p.m.: Contractions getting so painful that I have a hard time hanging on. The epidural is called in, and about 20 minutes later the contractions are so hard that I start throwing up.

11:30 p.m.: Anesthesiologist shows up to administer epidural, but has to pause between contractions. Epi finally in by 11:30, and by 11:35 I am sound asleep. Between being sick the week before (well, the nine months before, really) and the strength of the contractions, I am exhausted. Marc said that the contractions had been spiking between 40 and 50 on the intensity scale before the epidural, and after they were into the 100s. Good thing I got it when I did. I was at 4cms at 11:30.

11:30 p.m. - 3:30 a.m. March, 15 I dilated about 2cms per hour and threw up two more times. I was burning hot, and Marc kept having to put cold wash cloths on my head, face and neck, and feeding me ice. I was totally out of it, but could feel each contraction opening things up. I finally had three contractions that were very close together and successively harder, and felt the need to push, but couldn't make myself wake up and say something. The nurse came in to check me and asked if I was feeling pressure yet, and I told her I had been for about 10 minutes. She checked me and Marc joked about me being 11cms. The nurse said, "Uh, she actually is, and the head is right there. We need to call the doctor NOW."

The nurse grabbed one leg, Marc grabbed the other (just what he DIDN'T want to do again), and she told me to push very slowly and gently to stretch the skin. I probably could have pushed Baby out on the first go, but the nurse didn't want me to tear and the doc wasn't there yet. He arrived a little before 4 a.m. and told me I could push as I needed to.

At 4:07 a.m. our baby girl came sliding into the world. Marc just about passed out, and the nurse ordered him to go sit down so he didn't become a problem. The final result, though – our little Harper – was absolutely worth the preceding eleven hours … and 38 weeks.

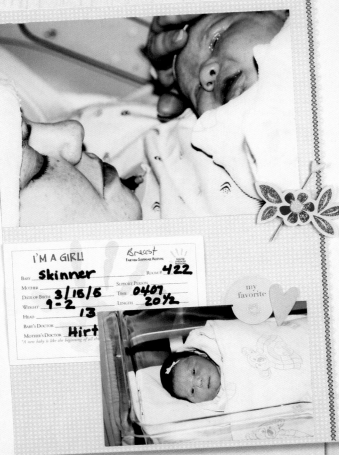

I'M A GIRL!
Breast

Baby Skinner Room # 422
Mother
Date of Birth 3/15/5 Support Person
Weight 9-2 Time 0407 Length 20½
Head 13
Baby's Doctor Hirt
Mother's Doctor
"A new baby is like the beginning of all things..."

my favorite

Whether you have one child or five, the story of their birth will always remain clear in your memory. But have you scrapped a birth story yet? When I wrote the story of my daughter's birth, I couldn't make it short enough for a layout. Sticking with the basic facts became the way to go. Use a timeline to journal about an event—maybe the weekend of your wedding or how you spent your holidays. Or use a timeline to mark several events in a year. Timelines are a wonderful way to hit the highlights without worrying about the overwhelming details.

Supplies: Cardstock (Bazzill); patterned paper (Pebbles); rub-on letters (American Crafts); glitter accents, ribbon (Making Memories); heart accent, pin (Heidi Grace); Misc: floss

My consolation prize

When your dream company came to call, inviting you to interview for a great position, we were both so excited. I think I was actually more excited than you. You had reservations … what if you interview and they tell you that you don't have enough experience? What if the offer is crap? What happens if you go to work for Red Hat, the company you've idolized for more than ten years, and it doesn't live up to expectations? But I encouraged you and helped you feel excited that *they* contacted *you* to interview, and that they saw your skills shining through enough to want to know more.

So the day of the interview came, and you found out that the job was even better than was implied. And the salary and incentive plan were phenomenal. And you received an email from Red Hat, saying an offer would be coming, before you even got on the plane to fly home. Wow. We were equally elated.

Then the job started. And in the first six weeks you worked for them, you were home about 12 days.

The job is great, and we're both still so excited about this opportunity and all that could happen from it. But sheesh … the *travel*! This is *not* what we were told!! And now you are getting ready to head out for another seven days.

But these flowers … on the day you returned home from your fourth state in five weeks, you stopped by the grocery to pick up something and surprised me by bringing home these amazing roses. They were seriously some of the best roses I've ever seen, even if they *were* from Cubs! You knew how hard the past five weeks had been on me, and you wanted to show me, in some little way, that you appreciated my support of your new endeavor, even if it meant I was stuck on non-stop solo kid duty for the foreseeable future.

These roses were my consolation prize for having to put in so many extra hours with so much less help so you can fly off and make your dreams come true. I'd rather have you home, someone to take the kids at the end of the day, someone to talk to in the evening about adult things. But I'll take the roses. For now.

These flowers said to me, "I may not be able to give a kid a bath or wash the dishes, but I do appreciate the fact that you are taking care of it all without me." They were a daily reminder that while I didn't anticipate playing the role of a single parent for the foreseeable future, I was playing a much larger role: that of a supportive wife. Look around the house. Is there an object that triggers an emotion in you? Find that object and see what thoughts it sparks.

Supplies: Cardstock (Bazzill); rub-on letters (Making Memories); buttons (Doodlebug, Making Memories); corner rounder (EK Success); Misc: Apple Garamond Light and Steelfish fonts, wire

Owie my...

backtummytushielegcrotchelbowfingerheadarmfooteyehair

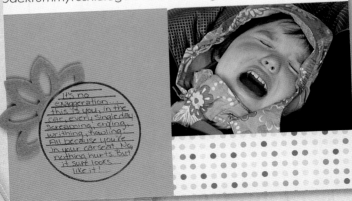

It's no exaggeration— this is you, in the car, every single day. Screaming, crying, writhing, howling. All because you're in your car seat. No, nothing hurts. But it sure looks like it!

My daughter is a hypochondriac. Something always hurts . . . usually at bedtime or while riding in the car. I didn't want to take the time to write a huge amount about this affliction, and realized that listing all of her common ailments was actually a better and more interesting way to express this topic. If you don't want to wait for your own words to come, use the words of others. Don't make journaling harder than it needs to be.

Supplies: Cardstock (Bazzill); patterned paper (KI Memories); chipboard letters (Zsiage); letter stickers (Doodlebug); flower (Queen & Co.); journaling stamp (Autumn Leaves); Misc: Century Gothic font, ink, paint, pen

PROBLEM SOLVED

"I get so stressed when I scrap because I worry so much about getting the formatting right and choosing the right font and fitting it on my page! How do I get over my fear and just write?"

I always start a page with the journaling, and then I fit the photos and art around it. On my pages, the words carry the most weight, so I want to know that I've said all I need to say before I consider what else will go on a page.

Type your journaling, and format it in a way that feels comfortable. Word processing programs make it so easy. Create a text box and give it the dimensions you want, then make your journaling fit. If your journaling ends up too long to fit on a page with photos, consider making a pocket to hide your journaling. Or format it onto several smaller pages and create a "book" on your page. As far as fonts go, I dare you to count how many layouts in this book use Apple Garamond Light! Scrappers are hoarders, and that extends to fonts. But having too much can lead to a paralyzing inability to figure out what to use. Stick with basic, easy-to-read fonts, and if you can find one or two favorites, all the better!

"Give or Take" was done at a crop, so my journaling had to be ready to go before I even thought about the final product. I typed up the words, formatted them to look nice and hit print. Instead of worrying about the journaling while cropping and chatting, I was able to spend my time playing with the design.

Supplies: Cardstock (Bazzill); patterned paper (Scenic Route); chipboard letters (American Crafts); letter stickers (KI Memories); buttons (Autumn Leaves); Misc: Garamond font

Regardless of who your audience is when you journal, writing down what you have learned along the way—be it life lessons or, like Sandra, "Random Tips" about something—is a great and quick opportunity to use your voice and get some thoughts on a layout. Use humor or honesty or simple observations, but use them in a way that gives personality to a basic list. Illustrate each tip with a good photo and give even more authenticity to your words.

Supplies: Patterned paper (CherryArte, Reminisce); letter stickers (Doodlebug); tag (K&Co.); chipboard accents (Junkitz)

Artwork by Sandra Stephens

Have you ever opened your mouth and heard your mother come out? It happens to me more and more often, especially as my kids get older. One day I said something that was so much my mom that I had to quickly write some thoughts for a layout. Whether you like it or hate it, turning into a parent is inevitable. And to document it on a layout is not only a great way to get another quick page done, but it's also a nice way to realize that maybe being like Mom or Dad isn't so bad after all.

Supplies: Cardstock (Bazzill); patterned paper (Pebbles); chipboard letters (Making Memories); sticker accents (Creative Imaginations, Heidi Swapp); felt (Fancy Pants); ribbon (Offray); Misc: Apple Garamond Light font, buttons

PersPective

Being a mother has given me a whole new perspective on what my mom went through in raising us. Things that I did when I was a kid that drove her – what I considered *unfairly* – crazy, I now see my kids doing. And yes, they drive me crazy. But truth is, perspective has made me respect my mom a whole lot more.

Maturity makes many things more clear. First of all, it helps us understand that we are where we come from. Our personalities are influenced by how we are raised, but what we don't realize is that our parents' personalities are influenced by how *they* were raised. Anything that comes at us as kids started waaaayyy before our parents.

Secondly, the things that we do and think as children look way different at the time than they do in hindsight. When I was young and was trying to mother my little sister, I got in trouble for it. My tone of voice was wrong, my tactics were wrong, everything was wrong. And I got so frustrated because I was just trying to help lay down the law. But now that I see my oldest doing the same thing to my youngest, I get irritated with him and try to enforce that he is not the parent; I am. And then I get a shiver and think, "Oh my goodness … I've turned into my mother."

And that's no longer a bad thing.

No mother is perfect. We're all bound to make mistakes and screw up our kids a little. But the fact that I'm a decent, productive, open-minded member of society makes me think that my mom actually didn't do too badly.

I appreciate the fact that I was raised to think for myself, take care of myself, not rely on others to give me the things I want from life. I was raised to be loving, compassionate, intelligent, appreciative of the arts, respectful of my surroundings, and to be a connoisseur of beautiful things.

Our relationship is so different now than it was when I was younger, and for that I'm thankful. My mom and I can talk like equals now, and we've actually become friends instead of just a parent-child relationship. I feel like she trusts my opinion and my experience more, and I trust her right back.

I love my mom, and regardless of what I remember about my childhood, she made me who I am today. So it must not have been as bad as I thought.

BEST LAID {not} PLANS

How hard can it be to get photos of an adorable eight-month-old girl in her first Christmas dress? Well, apparently, really hard.

I tried over the course of two weeks to get Harper into the studio, but each time, the universe threw something our way. I scheduled an afternoon appointment just after Thanksgiving, but that fell through, too. However, the lady at the studio said an appointment for the following morning had just opened up. Hallelujah!! Prime photo shoot real estate!

We woke up, dressed, and were in the car by 9:40 a.m., heading to the studio. But not five minutes into the trip, we found ourselves at a standstill, on a merge ramp, due to a major accident just under the overpass. And there we sat for 45 minutes, without budging an inch.

So returning home grumpy and frustrated, I thought, "To heck with the photo studio!" I pulled black fabric out of the closet, draped it over chairs in front of the dining room windows, sat Harp down, and started to shoot.

Then had to move her back onto the fabric.

And began to shoot again.

And had to beg her to sit still and look at Mommy.

And began to shoot again.

And watched her take off at full speed for the door, flashing her little be-stockinged booty at me.

Well, so much for that idea.

But at least I didn't have to pay for it.

OVERCOMING OBSTACLES

We all have stress and obstacles in our lives that get in the way of accomplishing tasks. Scrapbooking should not be an obstacle; it should be a reward and pleasure.

So how do we remove the stress of journaling to make the process of completing layouts flow more easily? The first thing to do is to stop putting so much pressure on yourself to be perfect. Your journaling doesn't need to sound perfect; imperfect journaling is better than no journaling at all. You don't need the perfect photo to write great journaling, nor do you need to include every detail. And who cares if your grammar and spelling aren't perfect! Unless you plan to get published at some point, your pages don't need to be flawless, just honest and interesting.

Perhaps you've passed the point of needing to be perfect, but you avoid writing anything personal for fear of someone reading it. We can work on that too! Don't let the fear of losing privacy keep you from writing, but know when to hide the words from public consumption.

Obstacles are put in our path to make us stronger and more resilient to them later on. Let's get to work overcoming them!

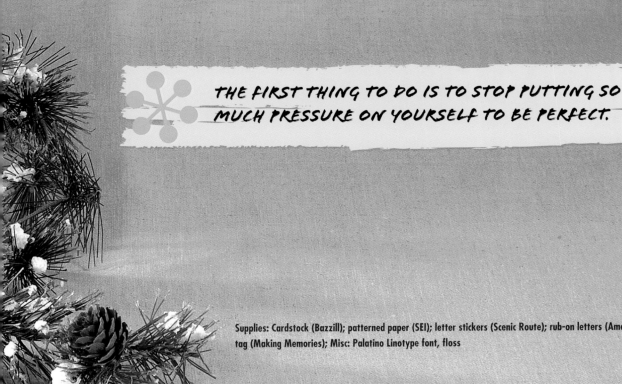

THE FIRST THING TO DO IS TO STOP PUTTING SO MUCH PRESSURE ON YOURSELF TO BE PERFECT.

Supplies: Cardstock (Bazzill); patterned paper (SEI); letter stickers (Scenic Route); rub-on letters (American Crafts); tag (Making Memories); Misc: Palatino Linotype font, floss

PERFECTIONISM

The goal of journaling is to record the story and your voice. Don't worry about perfection! Writing well and recording every detail are only optional.

It's what they do. Every time we visit during fishing months. From catching 11 fish in 20 minutes to catching a 24" catfish, Henry has definitely gotten the "Roush boy" touch from Grandpa!! 2004

grampa + HeNRy = FISHING!

I have many photos of my son and my dad fishing together. I debated making a layout for each time, and I debated creating a collage. In the end I went with cohesive photos and referenced different fishing outings in the journaling. There isn't a lot for me to write about their fishing—I don't know what conversations take place—so I didn't try too hard to fill in all the right words and thoughts. Just hitting the highlights in my journaling provides a story for the photos and something fun to read. Don't feel like you need to re-create every conversation or every feeling of every photo you take.

Supplies: Cardstock (Bazzill); patterned paper (Doodlebug); letter stickers (American Crafts, BasicGrey, Doodlebug); tags (Anchor Paper); ribbon (Offray); journaling stamp (KI Memories); Misc: ink, pen

we spent the first three days of our holiday in huntington with my family. because christmas is such a huge deal in the roush house, we opted to call xmas eve eve "faux 'xmas eve'" and real xmas eve became faux christmas. we did all the traditions, and the kids never knew the difference!

part one

CHRISTMAS

{in two parts}

part two

we arrived in indy on christmas eve, and the kids immediately got into the spirit of playing with cousins. real christmas morning was the good kind of chaos, with presents & lots of squeals from the kids. henry & harper were the only ones who believe in santa, but they never even noticed!

Holidays seem to be a huge struggle for many scrappers. You take the same photos and write about the same traditions year after year. It got so bad for me that I stopped scrapping holidays altogether! I realized, though, that my kids still love to see photos and read captions about Christmas. It really takes so little to create an authentic holiday page. Choose a couple of your favorite photos, jot down a few of the highlights and there you have it. No perfection required.

Supplies: Cardstock (Bazzill); patterned paper (Paper Salon, Scenic Route); chipboard letters (Heidi Grace); rub-on letters (American Crafts); felt ribbon (Queen & Co.)

When faced with scrapbooking a major event, there is a tendency to feel the need to capture every detail. Save these for a mini album and save yourself a lot of stress. Instead, connect with your feelings from the event. When Sue's parents celebrated their 50th anniversary, she used the opportunity to reflect on how the stability of their marriage has been a firm foundation for her own life. What will matter most in the long run isn't who attended the party or what they ate, but how 50 years of marriage created a sense of security for Sue.

Supplies: Cardstock; patterned paper, rub-ons letters (Dèjá Views); rhinestones (Target); Misc: Zurich font, ink

Artwork by Sue Thomas

TIMELESS

BLESSING

While watching you renew your wedding vows at your 50th anniversary party the love you share for each other was evident. I haven't had the same success with marriage and would have to live to be 91, and Greg 101, before I would be able to look back on 50 years of marriage. Despite not being in a position to replicate your feat, your timeless love has provided the steady backdrop to my life, allowing me to explore the world and discover myself knowing that the two of would be together and waiting for me at home. You may never realize what a blessing this has been in my life but because I had the privilege of growing up with you as parents I know how to love and will always be "home."

the autumn that wasn't

2007: Autumn approaches, and for the first time in months, we have three free weekends in the same month. And as luck would have it, they are all in our *favorite* month: October. Happy thoughts raced through our heads: Time to pick apples! Time to pick pumpkins! Time to go outside and take family photos on the grounds of the gorgeous Minnesota Landscape Arboretum! But wait. First it rains. For three weeks straight. And the wind blows. And the leaves barely change color because of summer's drought. And the leaves that do change color are immediately blown from the trees by the rain and wind. Then the rain tapers off for a day ... as I fly to Canada to teach for the weekend. And when I get home, it's beautiful outside ... but now Marc's gone. We manage to get away for a weekend for our anniversary ... and it rains. The whole time. Finally the rains end, there are a few pretty trees left, and ... it's October 27. Four days until Halloween, and in that time I have a photo shoot, Marc is traveling, then it's his birthday, and then it's Halloween. No time for apple picking, or pumpkins. Barely enough time to put together costumes.

It is sad, really. The one month in the whole year that we eagerly anticipate, the one season that makes all the others bearable, were major bombs in 2007. We need an Autumn-Do-Over, because this one just ... wasn't.

Many scrappers have good stories to tell but no photos to go with them, so they never create the page. That's silly! Let's say you have waited all year for a particular event—autumn, for example—and then the event didn't go as you planned. Well, that's a story to tell, isn't it? Don't dwell on the fact that you don't have perfect—or any!—photos. Don't worry that the plans you made for pages won't happen because the event wasn't what you hoped it would be. Journal what really happened; that's the authentic way to go.

Supplies: Cardstock (Bazzill); letter stickers, patterned paper (BasicGrey); rub-ons (Heidi Grace); Misc; Calisto font

While my dad and Kathy were visiting, I realized suddenly where my kids got their elf ears. Henry, Harper and my dad all have the same two different ears … one that's a little round, and one that sticks out a little more and has a slight elfin curve to it.

Huh.

So of course I had to get a photo of the three of them and their ears … *the photo for posterity*, so to speak. But the kids weren't cooperative. They moved, they made faces, they wouldn't turn just so.

And then there was this shot. Sadly, it was the best of the bunch. But I took it at the exact moment Kathy's flash went off on her camera. Henry was holding his ears out like some Super Beagle. Harper was making THAT face. And no one was looking at me.

Grumble.

Well, so much for that idea.

But you can still kind of see that the ears are all the same.

Kind of.

4.06

tHe idea tHat weNt AWRy

Scrappers have a tendency to think ahead. We dress our kids to match a scrap supply we just bought. We coordinate clothing to surroundings that will be in photos. We envision the perfect photo we want to take to go with the journaling we plan to write. But getting that perfect shot doesn't always happen. Sometimes the universe has other plans. Go with it anyway, or else do what I did on this layout: Tell about how reality waylaid your idea. There's definitely an authentic story to be found when you admit something didn't go perfectly!

Supplies: Cardstock (Bazzill); patterned paper (Sassafras Lass); chipboard letters (American Crafts); letter stickers (Doodlebug); digital frame (Designer Digitals); Misc: P22 Garamouche font

PRIVACY

A fear of losing privacy shouldn't keep you from journaling. There are lots of ways to keep your words hidden.

look inside

C

can U KEEP a secret?

I have secrets. Doesn't everyone? Not mind-blowing, earth-shattering secrets. Just normal everyday stuff. You know the kind that is slightly embarrassing so you would rather no one knew. Well don't tell anyone but here are a few of my slightly less embarrassing ones...

1. I'm afraid of the dark.
2. I don't like any of my food to touch.
3. I would eat chocolate cake for breakfast everyday if I could.

my sister's phone numbers.

'06 summer

Artwork by Crystal Jeffrey Rieger

Solve the problem of keeping things private by using hidden journaling. Write things down and tuck them away for your own peace of mind, but know they are there in case you ever want someone to know your secrets. Crystal designed this fun page to hold a few of her "slightly embarrassing" secrets; nothing too shocking, but personal enough that she's not ready to share them with the world. Journaling placed in small envelopes provides the privacy she needs, and the small bit of journaling on the page hints at the story.

Supplies: Cardstock; patterned paper (Anna Griffin, BasicGrey, Heidi Grace); letter stickers (Making Memories); rub-on letters (ChartPak, Heidi Swapp); acrylic letter, star accent (Heidi Swapp); clips (Making Memories, unknown); ribbon (Michaels, Wrights); staple accents (EK Success); Misc: button, floss, ink, pen

PROBLEM SOLVED

> "I feel like people will judge me for what I think and write, or they will laugh at me. How can I write about sensitive subjects without worrying what others will think?"

All I can say is don't be afraid! Don't let your fear of what others think keep you from writing things you feel. Do your family and friends love you? Then they'll still love you even if you are a bit honest on a scrapbook page.

I occasionally use my scrapbooks as therapy. I write the things I wish could be said out loud. Then again, I don't have much fear because no one ever asks to see my work. I know it'll stay private. And if there is something I don't want my kids to read, I'll keep that well hidden until a time when I deem it safe to reveal. What you say and how much you say on layouts is totally up to you. But if fear of others is stopping you from writing, then start a scrapbook that's for your eyes only. You can use your pages just to write and feel better, or you can use them as a conduit to a discussion that's long overdue.

The page "Lucky" came out after really thinking about how lucky my kids are to have my sister as an aunt. Becca and I weren't always close, but I can now admit that I was at fault for a lot of things. Apologizing on paper wasn't easy. And the reaction from my sister and our parents when they see this page could go a couple ways—bad and good—but I had to say what was on my mind without fear of their reactions.

My kids adore their Aunt Becca. And why wouldn't they? She's such a kid herself, always silly and doing goofy things. She has the energy and enthusiasm that any child would want to be around.

She started to visit us in Minnesota by herself when she was in college. It was always such a treat for Henry to have solid one-on-one time with one of his most favorite people, and I was glad that we were finally getting to know each other.

My sister is nearly 10 years younger than I am, so being close has always been tricky. I resented her appearance when I was younger because life had been a series of upheavals to that point anyway. Not long after she was born, we moved to Indiana, where being the New Kid in school led to years of unhappiness. I unfairly associated Becca's presence with much of that.

Then, when we were both finally old enough to have a relationship, I headed to college. Then marriage. When she was 13 and needed a big sister, I was 23 and starting my own life 600 miles away.

It's been tough to get close since then, but we do our best.

My kids think having her for an aunt makes them very lucky. And now I can add that having her as a sister makes me very lucky, too.

lucky

Supplies: Cardstock (Bazzill); patterned paper (SEI); latter stickers (Sonburn); metal accent (American Crafts); sticker accents (Heidi Grace); Misc: Century Gothic font, pens

Nature didn't make you my dad.

But God did.

So I guess it all worked out okay in the end.

Do you have strong emotions that you just aren't ready to put into words? Don't feel like you have to bare your soul on every layout. Sometimes the simplest words are the best. I created this lighthearted tribute to my dad, who adopted me when I was eleven. The page wasn't meant to carry the weight of a lot of words, yet the few words that are on the page say everything I want to communicate. There are ways to say what's in your heart without going too deep. Find the simplest path and start there.

Supplies: Cardstock, chipboard accent (Bazzill); brad, paint, patterned paper (Making Memories); Misc: 2 Peas Rickety font, ink, ribbon

Is THIS... THE best DAY OF THE WEEK?

we wait for that call... the one that says "i'm home." Then we all pile in the car & head to the airport, where we'll circle the terminal a few times (if there's luggage to wait for). Then we head to baggage claim & creep toward door no. 6, and then... there he is: DADDY! The one who makes everything better. And suddenly the week looks brighter.

DATE jan. 08 SIGNED me

Love @ 1st sight!

love

Things I love
- NWA flight alerts via email... seeing you at the curb... bringing you Home!

Some thoughts I keep to myself, as I'm sure you do too. This page is one of them. No matter how much I care about Marc's dreams, I have to say that having a husband who travels out of state makes for a long, long week. And the best time of that week is the moment we pick him up from the airport. Now, is that something I want to shout from the rooftops? No; I don't really want Marc to feel guilty about leaving. But my feelings are still worth noting on a layout. What are some thoughts you have that might be better left unsaid, but need to be recorded?

Supplies: Cardstock (Bazzill); journaling card, patterned paper (Collage Press); letter stickers (American Crafts, Collage Press); rub-on letters (American Crafts); sticker accents (7gypsies, Collage Press, Daisy D's); chipboard accents (K&Co., Scenic Route); pen (Uniball)

It has to be said that I hate my body. I hate what the past nine years have done to it. I hate that the simple, everyday act of getting pregnant caused so many adverse reactions in my physical appearance. The unexplained sudden gain of 20+ pounds in the final two weeks that worried my doctor enough to make her want to induce me ASAP. The onset of perimenopause symptoms that needed treatment, which put the brakes on my post-partum weight loss and put extra pounds on me. The diagnosis of post-partum depression that kept me from getting out of bed some days, and spending the next two years on antidepressants, which slowed my body's reaction to diet and exercise and caused further weight gain. Then doing it all over again for a second pregnancy.

I hate that I no longer care how I look, that I hate shopping, that I hate talking to my family about things like food and clothes and weight and life because I ultimately feel completely guilty of how ugly and unacceptable I am around their tiny perfectness. I hate that I cringe when Marc tries to hold me and touch me. I hate that I stick to dark or neutral colors because I feel like it makes me fade into the background. I just hate, hate, hate what I've become.

But it ends. Now. Now I get back to the gym. Daily. Maybe with a personal trainer. And I start taking my health and life seriously. And I shed all of the responsibilities that aren't critical and start putting myself first. I get back to that place where I'm okay with Me. And once I am? Look out. I will shop my brains out. And I will buy color.

i will have color again

If you're like me—and probably most other women—you have a constant sense of hating something about yourself. But that isn't something to share freely. Create a layout to give yourself permission to be completely open about how you feel (even if you never show anyone). Here I took on the very personal and depressing subject of body image. But I was determined to give myself hope, so I included pictures of the lovelies I can't wait to buy to reward myself. Can you use a page to inspire change in your life? Of course! Giving your goals a visual can help keep you motivated.

Supplies: Cardstock (Bazzill); patterned paper (Making Memories); letter stickers (American Crafts); letter stamps (Paper Studio); journaling tag (Jenni Bowlin); Misc: P22 Garamouche font, ink

THE STORY OF: Sandra

WhaT iF

COLEGIO PUERTORRIQUENO
DE NINAS

CALLE TURQUEZA,
GOLDEN GATE

CAPARRA HEIGHTS , P. R.

Sandra Gándara

open

Libertyville
High School
LIBERTYVILLE, ILLINOIS
1986-1987

Sandra Gandara '88
1012 Shari Lane
Libertyville, Il

At 16, I hated my parents. It was not because of "normal" teenage angst: not letting me go out with my friends, not letting me drive, curfew, limited phone use, etc...

I hated them for moving us 2,000+ miles away from our family and friends. In 1986, we moved from Rio Piedras, Puerto Rico to Libertyville, IL. I left behind my high school friends whom I had so much in common with. I left behind my grandparents whom I adored. I left behind my culture and the many things and places that defined me as a Puerto Rican. I still remember closing my eyes during takeoff because I refused to say goodbye to "my" island.

Moving to the States was a culture shock. I had to deal with speaking a different language (and, trust me, I sucked at it) and my new high school was unbearable. I went from a class size of 26 to 505 and there were days I didn't talk to anyone. My junior and senior years were very lonely ones.

What if we had never moved here? I'm positive I wouldn't have attended Purdue University. That means I wouldn't have met John and I wouldn't be the mom of Cassandra and Ian. Changes are extremely difficult but they've made me who I am today.

Thanks Mom and Dad for making the difficult decision. I know you wanted us to have more opportunities and you were right. As you usually are!

Artwork by Sandra Stephens

Sometimes you want your journaling to remain hidden not so much because it's private, but because it is in such stark contrast to the the rest of the page. Sandra's journaling is heavy and detailed. But the layout's design is simple and bright, and the title and picture play out the "What If" as much as her journaling does. Create a "What If" page of your own, with photos or stories showing before and after.

Supplies: Patterned paper, tab sticker (Fontwerks); kraft cardstock; chipboard letters, ribbon (Making Memories); round sticker (Scenic Route); envelope, tags (Paper Source)

Once Upon a Time

joy

... in a land not so far away, there lived a beautiful little girl. This little girl had a wonderful life, filled with playing with her older brother and wearing his hand-me-downs, running around outside and digging in the dirt, and obsessing over ladybugs and moths. She was a happy little girl and didn't feel there was anything missing from her life.

Then one day she went to the home of another little girl, and a whole new world appeared. She discovered dress-up clothes, jewelry and crowns, play kitchens and baby dolls. And this little girl's eyes grew wide and her smile grew broad across her sweet little face, which was adorned with a Bob the Builder bandage on her cheek.

Her mother saw the little girl's curiosity and joy, and vowed that day to bring more girly things into the home.

The very next day, a journey was made to the magical boutique known around the land as Target, home of all your heart's desires. The little girl and her mom went up and down the aisles until they saw it: the reason for their journey. A lavender and pink gossamer gown, covered with lace and glittery things. And what's more, there was a hat. And on the very next shelf, shoes and a matching wand.

Smiles and giggles were heard throughout the land as the little girl and her mother returned to their home and the gown was placed upon the girl's body. Instantly, a princess was born. And she grew stronger and more lovely every day. Though she still loved to dig in the dirt. Especially if she was wearing pink.

THE END

PART 2
Your Story
USE IT!

Now that you know how to find your words and make them your friends, let's get to work putting them to good use! Take a moment to look at the big picture: Why do you scrapbook? Is it to leave a legacy? Is it to preserve the memories of trips and holidays and events? Is it your therapy and creative outlet? The way you look at the "why" behind your scrapbooking will determine just what you should do with your words. For many scrappers, simply putting down photos, names and dates is enough. For others, though, scrapbooking is so much more. It's the story behind the story. But how do you get to that story?

What you choose to put in the pages of your own album is completely up to you. Be as chatty as you like, or keep it short, sweet and to the point. Be creative with your words and use them just as much as any decorative element or embellishment you put on a page. Or use your words to put down your very heart and soul, all your dreams and hopes and fears, regardless of whether anyone will ever read them. The point of journaling is to tell your story and the stories of your loved ones. The fun of journaling is to hop outside of the box and play with those stories any way you see fit.

Just to prove to you there is no one right way to tell your story, take a look at some of the many ways you can journal on a page:

1. Journal with lots of words or only a few.
2. Stick to making lists.
3. Use humor, or write to bring on tears.
4. Write like your audience won't be around tomorrow.
5. Turn information into a catchy classified.
6. Give stories a creative spin by writing fiction or haiku.

Whatever you choose to do with your words, remember that you are the author of your own story. What you decide to write and how you decide to write it are completely up to you. Just write; that's all I ask.

 THE POINT OF JOURNALING IS TO TELL YOUR STORY. THE FUN OF JOURNALING IS TO PLAY WITH THOSE STORIES ANY WAY YOU SEE FIT.

Not every girl would be swept off her feet by a bowl of kosher mini gherkins. But I'm not every girl.

I was seven months pregnant with Harper, sitting on the couch with Marc to relax after a long day, when Marc announced he was off to find a snack. Was I craving anything, he asked. Yeah, actually ... mini gherkins. Maybe about six.

So up he went, and a few minutes later he returned with a bowl of pickles. But not just any pickles ... pickles with their little pickle butts cut off.

Now, some girls go weak in the knees for a bouquet of flowers or a love note or some grand sweeping gesture. But not me. I'm all about the "Do you listen to me and hear me and remember what makes me *me?*" Knowing and acting on my little details and quirks – now *that's* romantic! And Marc ... let's be honest ... isn't so great at either type.

Which is why when he brought me that bowl of pickles, with their little hineys cut off, I started to cry. For the first time in all our years together he truly remembered something unique to me – I won't eat pickle butts – and acted on it. It was the most romantic thing he'd ever done for me.

That's either truly sweet or truly sad. It's all in how you look at it.

EMOTION

The difference between an average scrapbook page and a great one is its ability to pull in readers and tell them a story. It's even better if the page gets an emotion across in the process. Is the story a funny one? Make them smile. Is it a heartfelt one? Choke them up.

So, how do you accomplish voicing emotion successfully? Easy: By feeling it yourself when you are writing. Figuring out how to write with emotion is a trick that is hard to master, especially if writing doesn't come naturally to you. The key is to be honest. One thing that helps is to switch around the point of view from which you write. If you tend to write predominantly from a third-person point of view (writing as a narrative and using pronouns like "he said . . . " or "she was . . ."), switch things up and try first-person, writing from your own perspective, or second-person, in which you directly address someone. This helps make the act of writing much more personal and injects so much more emotion and depth.

And remember, perfection is not required when telling your story. Feel free to write like you talk, especially if you are relaying humor. Improper sentence structure and certain language are keys to finding your voice and all the emotion it conveys.

PERFECTION IS NOT REQUIRED. FEEL FREE TO WRITE LIKE YOU TALK, ESPECIALLY IF YOU ARE RELAYING HUMOR.

Supplies: Cardstock (Bazzill); patterned paper (Pebbles); photo corners (Making Memories); embroidered accent (Autumn Leaves); Misc: CAC One Seventy font

MAKE 'EM LAUGH

People love to laugh, so if humor is your forte, use it to inject real emotion into your journaling.

But I already bought THE dress

But I already bought the dress

You were shopping with friends and found this dress. You knew you had to have it so you put it on hold and took me back with you the next day to pick it up. When I asked where you would wear it, you told me you'd wear it to the prom. When I pointed out that you were 14 and styles might change by the time of the prom, you said that was the point; nobody would have a dress like yours in four years. Needless to say, you bought the dress. I came home from work the next day to find you lounging on the couch, eating snacks and watching a movie with the dress on. I know you must have thought "But I already bought the dress. Why is there no where to go to show it off!"

Artwork by Sue Thomas

Little kids are obviously great sources of funny stories, but teenagers can be just as good at making their parents smile. When Sue's daughter found the perfect prom dress—four years before she would actually need a prom dress—Sue wasn't keen on the idea of spending the money on something that probably wouldn't be worn. But her daughter's insistence that she would wear it, and then her follow-through, became a sweet story to share. Scrapbooking can give parents a different, and sometimes humorous, perspective. Looking for the humor in things is a far more fun way to go through life!

Supplies: Chipboard hearts and letter, letter stickers, patterned paper, ribbon (BasicGrey); Misc: AL Outdoors and Garamond fonts

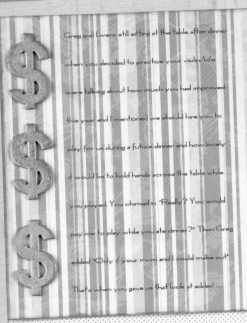

Greg and I were still sitting at the table after dinner when you decided to practice your violin. We were talking about how much you had improved this year and I mentioned we should hire you to play for us during a future dinner and how lovely it would be to hold hands across the table while you played. You chimed in "Really? You would pay me to play while you ate dinner?" Then Greg added "Only if your mom and I could make out." That's when you gave us that look at added ...

When you have a funny story to share, turn the words into a design element and use the story's punch line as your title. Doing so generates instant interest in the page, and it makes the rest of the story flow naturally. "That Will Be Extra," accompanied by a beautiful photo and dollar sign embellishments, becomes an irresistible title on Sue's layout. Find your funny story, then use the words to foster the mood of the page in the same way you would use design and product.

Supplies: Chipboard letters, patterned paper (Scenic Route); letter stickers (Me & My Big Ideas); chipboard accents (Fancy Pants, Maya Road); Misc: 2 Peas Squish font, ink, metallic paper, spray paint

THAT WILL BE extra

Artwork by Sue Thomas

Have you ever thought about writing to an inanimate object? Discussing your relationship with a favorite pair of shoes? Asking a purse for forgiveness because it's always stuffed so full? You'll find plenty of humor in absurd journaling. I took a look in my closet one day and realized my favorite color was being squeezed out in favor of a new color. And that started a whole page. What can you find around the house that is so familiar to you that you can actually talk to it? Find it, and then have some fun!

Supplies: Cardstock (Bazzill); die-cut shape, patterned paper (Piggy Tales); letter stickers (American Crafts); letter stamps (Fontwerks); button (Autumn Leaves); Misc: 2 Peas Rickety font, ink

greener pastures

I confess, I'm a cheater. For years my heart has belonged to butter yellow and orange, and I was a loyal and faithful devotee. But then one day my head was turned by army green. And I couldn't get enough. Army green sunglasses, army green crocs, army green socks, an army green parka. And then one day I found a blouse with a print of army green and... gasp...turquoise! Wait, turquoise? No way. Not me. But yes, it was true. I loved the shirt and discovered that turquoise and army green were a force too strong for me to resist. And I occasionally snuck in a little turquoise alone... socks, barrettes, t-shirts. If I was so lucky as to find something with army green and turquoise and some chocolate brown thrown in, well, let's just say it was nirvana.

Butter yellow and orange, I still love you. But I think our days of exclusivity are over.

ALL YOU CAN DO IS laUgh

where he left his pants

where he missed the bowl

where the drawer was apparently leaky

capture the moment   photo art   gallery   proof   evidence

So, have I ever mentioned that Henry sleepwalks? Usually when he really has to go to the bathroom but can't wake up enough to get himself there. He ends up wandering until we direct him to the toilet and help him go. Usually we make it. Sometimes we don't. The kid drinks too much at night and sleeps too hard. It's a problem.

Tonight was a whole new level, though.

Marc and I were downstairs watching *Lost* and I heard footsteps. I told Marc Henry was up. He said, "Huh." I said maybe he should go check to see if Henry was sleepwalking again so he didn't pee his pants. (I was at the computer ... Marc was just sitting there and could get up to Henry faster than I could.)

So Marc went up, I heard him talk to Henry a little, then he came back down. And he was laughing so hard there were tears in his eyes.

What, I ask.
You're gonna want your camera, says he.
Why, I ask.
Henry sleepwalked again, but you've gotta see where he peed.

(Catch that? *"Where he peed."* Three words that are never, ever good.)

Marc said he went upstairs and noticed immediately that the fridge door was open. He looked and Henry was standing in front of the fridge, eyes closed. Marc said, "What are you doing?" but Henry never opened his eyes. Then Marc noticed Henry's pants were down and the crisper drawer was open.

Yes.

My son sleepwalked into the kitchen, opened the fridge, dropped trou, opened the veggie drawer, and relieved himself. Completely. He was mid-stream so Marc had to just let him go.

Oh. My. Goodness.

So we had to empty out the crisper, throw away everything, clean and disinfect the lower half of the fridge and floor. Laughing all the way.

At least we laughed.

No more drinks for Henry after dinner. Ever.

The audience of this page is a general "you," directed to no one in particular. Because my scrapbooks are just as much for future generations as they are for me, I like to tell a narrative story. And using this implied "you" as an audience helps me remember to write in a narrative format. Don't feel like you need to limit your journaling to a certain audience. If you always write to Junior or Husband, shake it up and write to no one specific. Or write to yourself. Changing your audience on occasion can jumpstart your words.

Supplies: Cardstock (Bazzill); patterned paper (American Crafts, BasicGrey); letter stickers (BasicGrey); chipboard letters (Scenic Route); photo turns, sticker accents (7gypsies); brads (Impress Rubber Stamps); Misc: MS Mincho font

For $1.00 and unthinkable amounts of spit on our faces, we giggled away an entire morning. Who says money buys happiness? For my dollar, this was pretty perfect.

Sometimes all it takes are a few words to inject some humor. Don't feel like you need to force the funny . . . it will happen if you scrap stories that make you smile. This layout came about when I found photos from the morning we played with a bag of letters from the dollar store. The more I thought about how we played, the more I realized how much we had to lick those letters to get them to stick. Gross, right? But also a little funny. Adding a little humor is a much more interesting way to describe the photos than to just, well, describe them.

Supplies: Cardstock (Bazzill); patterned paper (American Crafts, Making Memories); felt trim (Fancy Pants); brads (American Crafts); Misc: Estrangelo Edessa font, floss

MAKE 'EM CRY

Everyone loves a good cry every now and then. Let people see the real you and write heartfelt words on a page.

...you can tell he's been down for a while. But, my God, it's so beautiful *when the boy smiles.*

Here he is...on the Fourth of July...smiling. Not a "mask for the world" kind of smile...but a real from-the-soul-Kavan smile. We had a blast that night... banging out...talking, laughing, grilling... annoying the neighbors with $100 dollars worth of screaming, sparkling, 'sploding "fireworks." After what Kav's been through the past few years, it was amazing to see him so genuinely happy. Just living in the moment. If only for a little while.

It all started because Kavan wanted to help people...clean up after a tornado...fill some sandbags to hold back a flood. And get some money for school...that too. Our hippie mom could barely believe it when he told her he was joining the Army National Guard. Boot camp was hard, but he made it through. Came out chiseled and grown up and ready for anything. Mom was a bit worried about what he would face as a man in the Army- but we were all assured by his higher ups that all would be well- "unless the sh*t hit the fan" chuckle, chuckle...what could go wrong in our happy little world? That was August of 2001.

Since then the world has tossed some bad stuff Kav's way...it definitely wasn't what he'd signed up for...but he didn't complain. During his year plus in Iraq- he and some buddies made signs for their Humvee that read "two weeks a year my ass"...these boys were National Guard...as in- supposed to be guarding our nation. Not dodging roadside bombs and guarding checkpoints in the 140+ degree heat of a desert over seas...for over a year.

He doesn't talk about it much... though I don't know that any of us have ever flat out asked what was it like? Because frankly- is there a right answer for that? And if there is...do we want to hear it? Every now and then he'll slip you pieces of his experience. I know that he spent his 21st birthday with his face buried in his helmet- hunkered down in a sandstorm. I know that he got a flat tire while leading a caravan- and had to stop to change it and that he was terrified...and I know that the driver who took over the lead hit a roadside bomb not long after. I know that he enjoyed the local children who visited him and talked about their lives, their world. I know that it made him sad when he got letters from US school children who drew pictures of army guys fighting and killing people. He understood that it was their way of showing support...but these were the things he saw in real life there. I also know we'll probably never hear the worst of it.

I can only imagine...or maybe I can't even do that. But it must have been bad. This is a boy who is bothered by next to nothing. Who lives in the moment and loves life so fully. And this haunts him. Seriously. It kind of comes and goes...though I'm sure the pain and sadness and just everything-is always there at least a little bit. It was hard around the election. It was hard when the bombings took place in London (he had been there just days before). It was hard when he was told that he had to do nuclear weapons training this summer...had to drive down south and train without his army buddies...on his own, basically. It was that news that brought him to the edge. That brought him home for the Fourth of July. He just needed to be home for a while before heading out. Home with mom. With the sibs.

He needed that. And we discovered we did too.

Iraq 2003

Artwork by Nisa Fiin

Whatever moves you to tears is the perfect thing to share with whole-hearted, emotional journaling. And who cares if it isn't something that would move everyone else to tears; these words are for you. Nisa's layout featuring photos of her smiling brother may not strike you as one that would bring tears, but then you read her journaling. Nisa writes with such eloquence and love. And the fear that her brother will be changed by the events he has witnessed is tangible in her words.

Supplies: Patterned paper (Autumn Leaves, Mara-Mi, Scenic Route, Scrapworks); rub-ons (7gypsies); ribbon (May Arts); bookplate (Jo-Ann); Misc: contact paper

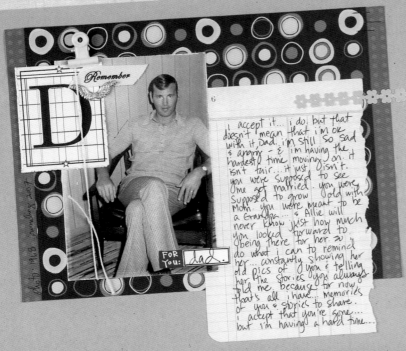

I accept it... i do. but that doesn't mean that i'm ok with it, Dad. i'm still so sad & angry - & i'm having the hardest time moving on. it isn't fair... it just isn't. you were supposed to see Ome get married. you were supposed to grow old with Mom. you were meant to be a Grandpa... & Allie will never know just how much you looked forward to being there for her. so i do what i can to remind her... constantly showing her old pics of you & telling her the stories you always told me. because for now that's all i have... memories of you & stories to share. i accept that you're gone.... but i'm having a hard time...

FOR YOU: dad.

Somehow, it's easier to deal with loss through writing than other forms of expression. For those who don't enjoy showing a lot of emotion, putting your heart and sadness on paper is a safe environment in which to grieve. Nicole addresses her father directly in her journaling for this layout. In it, she lists reasons she can't get through the grieving process. Have you suffered a personal loss? Is there something with which you can't find resolution? Write it down, and address the situation. The more emotion you feel while writing, the better you will feel afterward, and the truer your page will be.

Supplies: Cardstock; patterned paper (American Crafts, KI Memories); transparency (Hambly); cardstock monogram (Jenni Bowlin); clip, letter stickers (Making Memories); trim (Doodlebug); twill (7gypsies); sticker accent (Fontwerks); Misc: twine, vintage ledger paper and wings

moving on

Artwork by Nicole Harper

The scariest thing about loving someone so much is the thought of losing them. The very thought of having to go through the process of watching a loved one suffer from a disease prompted this outpouring of emotion. What brings tears to your eyes just thinking about it? Try to put words to your emotions. Do you know someone who's gone through the experience? Try to put yourself in their shoes as you search for the right words. You'll be surprised by how much empathy and emotion you feel.

Supplies: Cardstock (Bazzill); patterned paper (October Afternoon, Sassafras Lass, Scrapworks); letter stickers (Basic-Grey); die-cut paper, word stickers (Making Memories); rub-on border (Hambly); brad (Queen & Co.); Misc: Apple Garamond Light font, ink, paint, watch face

I want more time.

love

perfect

lifetime

What on earth would I do if I knew we had only days, hours, moments left together? What would I say? Would I want to just be quiet and hold you? Would I want to say everything that hasn't yet been said? Would I want to kiss you until your last breath? Would I step away so the kids could have their time? Would I share you with your family? Would I be strong? Would you?

The imminent or subsequent loss of a spouse or parent to cancer has been all around us for the past couple of years. And each time one passes on, I start to wonder what I would do if in the same situation. The thought gives me chills and brings tears to my eyes, and yet I feel thinking about it is an exercise in disaster management. My *Worst Case Scenario* training. You tease me that I constantly think of the "What ifs," but what if I didn't? I don't handle spontaneity well.

You are everything in the world to me. Well, you and the kids. And without any of you, I would be lost. Rudderless. Days would be pointless. Life would be anticlimactic.

But if you left in a way that gave us time to digest the situation, would that be any less painful than something unexpected, simply because I would have the time to make plans and get my feet under me? Or would my heart break more and more each day until there was nothing left in me?

How do you say goodbye to the love of your life? How do you fill only moments with enough words and love to last a lifetime?

I pray daily, fervently, that neither of us ever, ever, ever has to experience that kind of loss. Of course every married couple hopes that they live to be 95 together, and fall asleep one night holding hands and never wake again. That would be the ideal, right? But truth is one of us will leave the other. I just can't imagine that happening until we've had half a century or more together, and we can safely say goodbye with a smile on our hearts that our lives were well lived and well loved.

We have a plan, you and I. Cremation. I'm claustrophobic, and there's no way I'm going to put you in a box where you would be cold and alone. (Yes, I DO understand that you aren't really going to be there, but still. Thanks for humoring me.) And upon the time that we've both passed on, our kids will shake our ashes together and let us fly somewhere we both love ... the North Shore, maybe. Or the coast of Maine. Maybe they can fly some of us to a mountain in Quito, just for you.

But that's the Best Case Scenario. That occurs many, many years down the road, after our long life together. Because there's no way I can possibly love you enough in less than 60 years to call it good.

Please. Marc, God, whoever can fulfill this prayer; let us stay together until we're old and wrinkly. I can't possibly say goodbye any earlier than that.

PROBLEM SOLVED

"I know how important it is to write heartfelt journaling, but I'm not the mushy type. How can I get my emotions across in a way that doesn't sound insincere?"

This can be tricky. You want your family to know how much they mean to you, you want your friends to know how much you appreciate them, and you want so badly to capture the true essence of how you feel. But if flowery language and terms of endearment don't come naturally to you, trying to write them won't ever sound the way you intend.

One surefire way to know if your journaling sounds like you is to read it out loud. If you can say it easily and you don't stumble over phrasing and aren't grossed out by the words you chose, then you did a good job. Pretend you are actually talking to your intended audience. Will they feel your love? Will they get that you're being sincere?

My journaling on "I Miss This Boy" is my way of being heartfelt. Some background sets up what I'm about to say, and then I go into how I miss my son being little, because the years have gone so fast and he's such a different person now. But just when I risk going into sappy territory, I add a little humor, something to lighten up what I'm saying and remind the reader, "Yeah . . . this is still me."

There are so many things I could say about these photos … about how I had to bribe you with a new Thomas train piece if you made it down the aisle; about how you were gung-ho to be a ring bearer until the very minute you had to walk, and then you totally lost it and cried all the way to the altar (to be fair, you DID make it all the way); about how as soon as we got to the reception, you grabbed your Gameboy and were instantly relaxed and fine and completely yourself.

But all those details are just details. And they are now almost four years old and seem so far away. At the time we thought you were so big and so grown-up, because technically you WERE big (always in the 95th–100th percentile), and you WERE grown-up … being so smart fooled everyone into thinking you were older. You were our only child at that point, so we treated you as an equal. It didn't occur to us that you were only four.

I now see how small you were in your tuxedo, and how you were trying so hard to entertain yourself through the interminable process of preparing for a wedding, and how you were, I'm sure, trying to convince Daddy that you still needed a Thomas piece even though you cried through your job. Such four-year-old moments. And it makes me smile and grow teary with nostalgia for this little boy who now seems so far away. We had a good thing going and life was so sweet at that point. I wouldn't change anything about where we are now as a family, but I do occasionally miss the boy you were then.

Then I noticed the photo of you with the Gameboy and I realized: *never fear* … I still have that boy.

Supplies: Cardstock (Bazzill); letter stickers (American Crafts, BasicGrey); border sticker (My Mind's Eye); lace accent (K&Co.); rub-ons (7gypsies, BoBunny); button (Autumn Leaves); paint (DecoArt, Making Memories); Misc: Book Antiqua font

I now know fear. Fear so cold it ripped out my heart and filled my stomach with lead. Fear so intense it felt like it lasted an hour, when it was probably only a minute or less. Fear so complete I wanted to scream at the top of my lungs and stop the world.

I lost Harper.

It took only a second. I was watching her and Henry like a hawk, like I always do. I never look down, I never look away, I never assume the world is safe. But on this day I was with one of my best friends, a friend I hadn't seen in more than three years. And her kids were playing with my kids and everyone was well. Sandra and I were talking, and I was watching, and I could listen to her stories and watch my daughter playing by the big kid Legos all at the same time. I can multitask well.

Then Sandra said something, I glanced at her to respond, and I turned back to Harper. It took less than five seconds. But when I looked back, Harper wasn't there. Thinking perhaps she'd squatted down to find a Lego, I didn't instantly worry. Then I got up, said I'd be right back, and went over to find my girl. But she wasn't by the big kid Legos. So I walked to the side of Legoland, but she wasn't there. So I called her name. Loudly. Like she would actually answer me or come running. I called her again. I saw Henry and yelled, "Find! Your! Sister!" I took off running into the Legoland store, ran to the front of the store, looked down every aisle. I saw my friend get up and start looking. I was panicked. I felt like ice. I felt like my eyes weren't seeing anything and I wouldn't recognize Harper even if I looked right at her.

I prayed.

I ran back out into the play area. She wasn't there.

I ran back into the store. And there she was. Reaching for a box of Legos.

My. God.

I grabbed my girl and held her so tightly. Every possible scenario of what could have happened ran through my mind, and I gratefully thought, "It didn't happen!" She was there. She hugged me back. She had no idea how scared I was, how much worry she caused, how fast she is.

I held it together. I didn't cry or fall apart. I just said, "Whew! She's quick!" But my friend knew. She knew I was trembling. She knew I was not strong enough to deal if something had happened to my girl. We didn't speak of it, because what mom wants to say those thoughts out loud? We just went on with our day, took our kids on rides, hugged good-bye when our time was over.

Then I bought my kids a snack and we went home. Like any normal day. And we never talked about how I lost Harper. I couldn't say those words out loud. Not then.

It was too real. It was too close.

day i lost her

Every parent knows the answer to "What is your greatest fear?" Of course, it's the fear of losing a child. One day I lost Harper for about 30 seconds . . . the longest 30 seconds of my life. Sharing your fears on a scrapbook page can put words to your fear so that you never have to speak of it. That is the reason behind this page. I needed to get out the words and I needed to share what happened . . . maybe for no other reason than a justification for my vigilance in watching the kids!

Supplies: Cardstock (WorldWin); patterned paper (BasicGrey); chipboard letters (American Crafts); letter tabs (Autumn Leaves); rub-on (Imaginisce); Misc: Bookman Old Style font

---

I've mentioned that journaling can be therapeutic, right? Take the hardest thing you've ever dealt with and let it out on paper. Find some peace in getting it out; find some perspective in getting it written. It can be easier said than done, and I realize that, but it does help. When I miscarried after more than a year of trying for a baby, I thought it was a hurt that would never go away. But writing to the baby I'd never know helped me calm down, breathe and say goodbye. Use the minutes you spend writing to process your feelings.

Supplies: Cardstock (Bazzill); patterned paper (We R Memory Keepers); letter stickers (Making Memories); Misc: Book Antiqua font

---

Before I became a mother, I would have never understood how a woman could completely fall in love with a baby she'd never seen or held. But today I sit here with my heart breaking because I did love you so very much, and you left my life much too soon.

Ten days. That's all the time it took for me to know you were there, love you and want you, and then say good-bye. It's going to take me much longer than ten days to get used to the idea of a life that doesn't include you. We wanted you and dreamed of you and tried for you for a year and a half, and you surprised us with your existence at the most perfect time possible. Pregnant in the spring and summer, walks around the lake while holding my beautiful belly, looking forward to my favorite month, October, with one more date to eagerly anticipate. A fall baby, a little someone to share with family during the holidays and snuggle on cold winter days, a little person to round out our threesome ... the whole idea was wrapped in shiny fairy dust and twinkle lights. It was ideal. But it wasn't meant to be.

I wonder why God would finally grant me a baby after all those months of trying, only to take you back after ten days. Where is the fairness in that? Is it to tell me my body does indeed still work but this isn't the right time? Is it to make me see once and for all that I should be content with the one child I was given? I have no idea what my message is in all of this. I'm not sure I'll ever understand. The only thing I do know is that I hurt as if I had known you forever. You were a part of me, a biological element of my body, and I knew the very moment your little spirit disappeared from me. The sense of emptiness was overwhelming, and still is a couple of days later. How does a mother who wants a child so badly ever really forget the little life that wasn't completed?

I take great comfort in the fact that I have your brother. He is wonderful and perfect and also loved you very much, in a way only a four-year-old can express. He named you the very day I told him you were inside of me (*Junior* for a boy, *Bob* for a girl), he'd taken great pride in patting you gently, and he asked almost daily if he could sing you a song. It breaks my heart to think of him not getting the chance to know you. He's such a loving, gentle, empathetic soul, and I truly hope someday you will return so you can know each other.

I do miss you, little one, and I always will. You are welcome in our lives whenever you are ready. And if that day never comes, please wait for me in heaven so I can know you then. I love you even though we never met face to face. I know you are beautiful, wherever you are, and I'm so glad I had you in my life for these past ten short days. I selfishly pray that you will return to me very soon, but I need to accept that may never happen. You went to heaven as a loved, wanted soul, and I hope that love surrounds you with the warmest light.

Be well, my sweet. And know always that I love you and miss you with all my heart.

I miss you

UNIX REVIEW.COM

Shell Corner: Disk Space Checking wit...

Hosted by Ed Schaefer

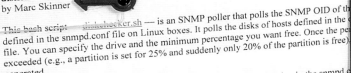

diskchecker.sh
by Marc Skinner

This bash script diskchecker.sh — is an SNMP poller that polls the SNMP OID of th... defined in the snmpd.conf file on Linux boxes. It polls the disks of hosts defined in the ... file. You can specify the drive and the minimum percentage you want free. Once the per... exceeded (e.g., a partition is set for 25% and suddenly only 20% of the partition is free)... generated.

I suggest monitoring all partitions. Include the disk partition information in the snmpd.c... hosts you want to monitor in the diskchecker.conf file. If you wanted to monitor the disk... host 10.10.10.5 and wanted to be alerted if the available disk space on partition /var had... you would follow the examples below. Remember the % listed in the snmpd.conf file is... minimum disk space free before the threshold is exceeded.

You're the guy who practically failed his SATs. You're the guy who never reads, and writes even less. You're dyslexic. And yet you go and invade my turf by getting *published*!! Granted it was in a Linux journaling and half of it was in code, but still ... you wrote the code.

I may be jealous, but I'm also darn proud.

Miracle

THE LONG AND SHORT OF IT

Sometimes less truly is more. And sometimes what you have to say can't be limited by a pre-sized journaling block. The process of writing and editing your journaling is just as much a matter of taste as a lesson in knowing when to say "when."

In some instances you can write a page or more of journaling about a specific topic, but when you sit down to read the final draft you realize the whole thing boils down to a main thought. Sometimes you want to include a lot of information but it looks too text heavy and reads too dry. In these instances, just write a little! Include some of the facts in a sidebar or write something brief on a tag and use it as a design element.

Then again, sometimes every word really is needed to convey the story. Maybe you need to address the audience with a little background to the story. Or maybe there is a lesson learned that needs to be shared. Feel free to write and write! Just as you don't want to bore the page with unnecessary writing, you also don't want to write too little and fail to bring the story to life.

Write what you want to write, then put on your editor's hat and see if you've said too much or too little and adjust accordingly.

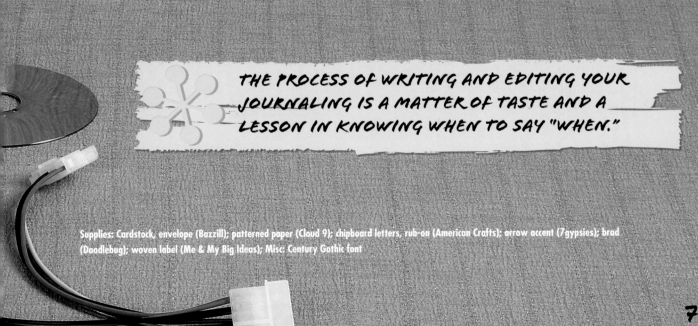

THE PROCESS OF WRITING AND EDITING YOUR JOURNALING IS A MATTER OF TASTE AND A LESSON IN KNOWING WHEN TO SAY "WHEN."

Supplies: Cardstock, envelope (Bazzill); patterned paper (Cloud 9); chipboard letters, rub-on (American Crafts); arrow accent (7gypsies); brad (Doodlebug); woven label (Me & My Big Ideas); Misc: Century Gothic font

LOTS TO SAY

When lots of words are needed to convey the story, feel free to write and write! Just be sure that the words are really needed to bring the story to life and look for ways to make the text seem less daunting for readers.

Keep the gas tank @ 1/4 or more! Play in the Rain. Don't let anyone intimidate you. Weigh the RISKS vs. the benefits. Tell someone you ♥ them. Know you CAN. Learn to drive a stick shift. Pay off your credit cards! Read A LOT!! Stand up for your children. Small weddings are fabulous! TRUST! You are loved! Travel A LOT! Be independent. Explore! Be compassionate. Stand up for yourself. "No" is an acceptable word. Do not marry anyone who is not kind and respectful. Your house does NOT have to be. PERFECT! THINK! Don't judge anyone because of their Religion. Your wedding day is NOT the most important day of your life. Wait to have kids. Never floss your teeth @ the table. Find your voice. Set up a good retirement plan – even if you are a stay @ home parent. Do not apply makeup while @ the table. It is ok NOT to have children. It is ok NOT to get married. Wear sun screen. Share. WASH YOUR HANDS! Table manners are very important! Drink lots of water. Take your vitamins!

Donate Locally.
Don't Speed.
Have FUN!
Be careful!
Take your cell phone.
Cherish Friendships.
Learn Your Options.
Record + Share your Stories.
Pay attention to expiration dates

MOTHER KNOWS BEST

Learn to Sew.
Accept Loss.
Don't smoke.
Exercise.
♥ Love each other.
Just be NICE.
Use common sense.
Ask Questions.
Find Answers.
Do not be hard

on yourself. Cherish those who are close to you. Don't risk your life for something stupid. Think about how your actions will effect someone else. You do not have to have a man/woman in your life at all times. Being alone is good too! Don't wear anything with writing across the butt. Your butt crack should be contained in your pants! Your kids will drive you nuts... its normal. Be a realistic weight. Learn how to pay it forward. Learn about other cultures. Trust your instincts. Follow your dreams! Find your passion. SPEAK UP! Understand finances. Know how to buy a house. Stand up for the underdog. Stay out of debt!! Save yourself... don't wait to be saved. Understand your healthcare. Tolerate NO abuse. Have fun but be careful! I Love you! xo Mom

Artwork by Catherine Feegel-Erhardt

Catherine came up with a clever way to get a lot of journaling on a page and still give it a beautiful design. She created a background out of beautiful layers of paper and transparencies, and then she slid the layout into a page protector and wrote her journaling directly on it. Clever! You can adapt this idea for a little journaling or a lot. Either way, it makes a powerful statement.

Supplies: Transparency (Hambly); patterned paper (Sandylion); label stickers (7gypsies); pen (Sharpie, Tsukineko); Misc: page protector

Killbear Provincial Park, Lighthouse Point, July 11, 2007

Yup! Pretty much talking to myself when I said that to the kids, but even as I said it smiled 'cause I know (as most moms do) that no matter how hard small children 'try' to stay dry near the waters edge it is near impossible!! It started innocently enough by standing close to the edge but then they 'needed' to jump from one rock to the other...

promise [NOT] to get wet...

Next thing they were completely soaked from the knees down but totally having the time of their lives 'cause they got away with duping mommy again!!

What is a mom to do except sit back and watch them enjoying their childhood. After all, it is just a change of clothing to have them all fixed up & that is nothing at all.

Artwork by Crystal Jeffrey Rieger

If you scrap a smaller size—not the 12" × 12" (30cm × 30cm) standard—it can be hard to fit in a lot of journaling. Borrow this trick from Crystal: Place your photos, title and embellishments on the page, then use the white space around them for journaling. As your writing moves from one block of space to the next, your story naturally continues with the photos.

Supplies: Patterned paper (A2Z, Sassafras Lass); letter stickers (American Crafts, office supply store); rub-on brackets (American Crafts); tag (Every Jot & Tittle); brads (Stemma); Misc: ink, pen

I'm a big fan of repetition in writing, especially if it's used to keep the subject cohesive when it's in danger of veering off onto a tangent. It also helps break up a lot of text and make it more readable. On this page, each little paragraph starts with the italicized words "I waited." Using those words ensured that each new thought followed the theme of the page: Waiting. If you struggle to keep the theme of your page solid, this is a great way to accomplish continuity.

Supplies: Cardstock (Bazzill); patterned paper (Chatterbox, SEI); letter stickers (American Crafts, Heidi Grace, Making Memories); cardstock accents (Heidi Grace); Misc: Apple Garamond Light font

worth THE wait

I waited a long time for this room, and thought – month after month when I didn't get pregnant – that I'd never get the chance to create another room for a baby.

I waited more than 20 weeks before starting plans for the room because I wanted to know whether I was creating a room for a boy or a girl. This time around I wanted a room that was specific and perfect.

I waited to start working on the room until I found the inspiration – vintage reproduction nursery rhyme posters. Once I had the starting point, I designed the bedding and found the fabric that matched what I had in my mind. Then I had to find the perfect touches in the colors that would bring it all together.

I waited until the week before you were born to actually sit in this beautiful, finished room. Your Grandma Lawrence sewed the bedding and window treatments, so I had to wait until they arrived from Illinois. I had to wait for your dad to do many projects, and finally had to haul my eight-months-pregnant self up a ladder to paint just so it would get done. I had to wait for time, money, deliveries … all of which finally came together at the very last moment.

The instant the last picture was hung, I smiled and felt perfectly at peace. And this room brings me peace still, because now you are in it. And it's your room.

And I no longer have to wait.

When I have a lot to say, I prize my words more than page design. On this layout, all the words had to be there, so I typed them and formatted the journaling to fit a 12" × 12" (30cm × 30cm) page. Because text took up most of the space, I limited the design elements. If you have a story that's worth a lot of words, it's OK to leave off all the embellishments you usually use. And if you don't have a large format printer, fill an 8.5" × 11" (22cm × 28cm) page with words and add it to a larger page.

Supplies: Cardstock (Bazzill); stamps (Fontwerks); rub-ons (Heidi Grace); Misc: Apple Garamond Light font

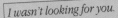

I wasn't looking for you.

I was hoping for someone not too tall, longish hair, maybe some facial scruff. Fishermen sweaters and Birkenstocks and a kayak strapped to the roof of his car. Someone who would swing in a hammock with me while we shared passages from whatever book or newspaper we were reading. Someone with whom I could sit in an Adirondack chair overlooking the water and split a bottle of wine. Someone to share thoughts on politics and literature and broad ideas. Maybe a professor or a nature guide.

And then I looked up one January morning and saw you. Tall, lanky, wearing a silver chain that looked like … a chain. A jock who could dunk basketballs and had a wardrobe consisting of wind pants, weird graphic t-shirts, and strange sneakers. Someone who would rather watch the Bulls game with the guys than attend a chamber music concert to which we had tickets. Someone who couldn't care less about literature, politics, a bottle of wine, but could talk passionately about Unix and programming in C++ and this amazing new operating system called Linux.

And for you, I fell hard.

But over the years, I discovered something wonderful. You love to fish. You love to camp … and the *REAL* way – hiking into the wilderness and living off nature. You love to grow scruff.

You are still a geek. You still won't share a bottle of wine with me or read a book. Your basketball days are over, and thankfully you've traded in Air Jordans for North Face. And now you actually prefer an orchestra to a basketball game.

You aren't at all the guy I thought I wanted. But luckily God knew what I needed. You are the patient, pragmatic voice at the end of a crazy day. You are full of light when I spiral into the dark. And 6'4" is pretty handy now and then.

I have been continually surprised by you. And now I am so thankful that, for whatever reason, a tall geek-jock in turquoise wind pants caught my eye that January day.

And life has turned out better than I could have imagined.

NOTES:
milmarc 1993
marc after fishing 2007

Sweet girl, I feel something so special for you. What you are going through in your young life … I've been there before. I know the future that could await you: the questions, the emotions, the confusion, the curiosity, the divided loyalties, the admiration, the gratefulness, the little bit of you that will always feel lost.

One thing I hope you always know is that your mom tried everything in her power to make things different, better. She put in more heart and effort and work and prayer than any of us thought was possible. Her strength and faith moved us all. But in the end, we felt sadness that there wasn't the outcome for which she'd hoped, and relief that it was finally over.

She deserves your respect for daring to find happiness and giving you both the life you deserve. My prayer is that one day, when she's ready, she meets a nice man who thinks the world of her and adores you. It can happen, and right now I know she isn't ready to even think of that, but I'll keep praying for her.

This layout says a lot but is formatted in a way that keeps it from feeling text heavy. By alternating the alignment of the paragraphs, I created room to add photos and design elements without having to worry about the weight of one large journaling block. Just because you have a lot to say doesn't mean you can't play with design. Try different ways to format your words, and see if doing so inspires different ways to design the whole page.

Supplies: Cardstock (Bazzill); patterned paper (BasicGrey, KI Memories, My Mind's Eye, Sassafras Lass); letter stickers (American Crafts, BasicGrey); brads (Doodlebug); rub-ons (Fancy Pants, October Afternoon); rhinestones (Heidi Swapp); dimensional paint (Ranger); Misc: button

When I was about your age, I went through the same thing. My mom tried to make things better, but ultimately she had to leave and take a leap of faith that things could be better. In the big picture, I don't blame either of my parents; they were ill-matched from the beginning. And both were later able to find the perfect person. My stepdad has been nothing less than *Dad* since I was five; I've never once considered him "step." And I adore my dad's wife more than I can say.

One blessing is that you are young. You won't really have any memories that life used to be different. And at some point you'll look at your parents and think, "How were you ever married?!" But you won't love either of them any less. In fact, you'll love them more because they are happy, and they gave you a happier life by letting go. And any time you fee confused or feel like you don't understand, call your Aunt Michele. I'll always love you and be there for anything you need.

PROBLEM SOLVED

"I tend to leave the journaling for last, but then I run out of room. How can I make sure I have enough space to say what I want to say?"

If you really want to tell a story, I suggest you rearrange your process for creating layouts. I rarely start a layout without prewritten or printed journaling. I would rather make the page fit the story than vice versa. If you are a die-hard hand-writer, write your journaling on a separate piece of paper. Use this to judge how much space to leave for journaling. You can rewrite your journaling on your layout or just adhere the separate piece to the layout. Typing up your journaling allows you to format and spell check all at once, and you can print it directly onto your background page before you add anything else. You can also preprint the journaling to take with you to crops.

Although I created the page "Game Ending Injury" while at a crop and I hadn't done any journaling ahead of time, I still designed the layout with the journaling first in mind. I left a large space for journaling. Then, when the time came to write, I gave some thought to what I would say so that I was sure to fill the alotted space but not run over. I also had predetermined what part of the story I would tell. Had I gone with the whole story, the journaling would have been much longer.

almost a

game-ending INJURY

there is a tragic story behind this photo. one about me and you and a shopping cart wheel. one about your first trip to the ER, you almost passing out and me throwing up. one about the sad realization that i'm not "fun mom." but the real story behind this photo is that mere hours after major injury, still baked on pain-killers & lacking a useable index finger, you still

5.04

{played your video games.}

what a trooper.

Supplies: Cardstock (Bazzill); patterned paper (Crafters Workshop, Creative Imaginations, Sandylion); letter stickers (American Crafts); rub-on letters (Reminisce); felt (Fancy Pants); rhinestones (Heidi Swapp); bracket stamp (7 gypsies); brads (Making Memories)

KEEP IT BRIEF

Journaling is not synonymous with lots of words. It's okay to keep it brief. And sometimes that's necessary to make an impact with your story.

1998

F r i e n d s h i p

friendship

celebrate

You met at Kid Stop the summer before first grade. From that time on, the two of you were inseparable. Your first grade teacher let me know that Alyssa, who was always a bit advanced in school, was turning in work for both of you so that you would have more time to play together. While the thought was sweet, I had to make the choice to separate the two of you at school. So for second and third grade you were in different classes, and still the friendship remained solid.

2003

enjoy

T h r o u g h   t h e   Y e a r s

You were back together in the same class for fourth and fifth grade. You also had Girl Scouts, Harry Potter and Just for Kix to further cement the relationship. But then, at the end of fifth grade we made the decision to move about an hour away. Shortly after we moved, Alyssa's family bought their first home almost an hour the other direction. I was sure your long distance relationship would be short lived. I should have known better. Telephone calls, My Space connections and week long summer get-togethers (often involving Harry Potter) have kept the two of you together despite the distance. I think the two of you have somehow found a way to ensure your friendship continues to grow through the years.

smile

2006

Artwork by Sue Thomas

At first glance, this page appears to have a lot of journaling. But compared to how many words it would take to tell the whole story of a friendship, two paragraphs is really not much. Sue condensed years of memories and used photos from the time periods to build a map through the years. She also chose to focus on the point that this friendship has withstood so many things, and for that, only the highlights are necessary.

Supplies: Cardstock; chipboard arrows (Heidi Swapp); felt flowers (Queen & Co.); epoxy flower (EK Success); number stickers (Chatterbox); word tiles (Target); scalloped rotary cutter (Fiskars); Misc: 2 Peas Submarine and AL Songwriter fonts, ribbon

no point in denying it--you're still a complete girly-girl.

never enough sparkle and shine for your taste,

because in your opinion--

when it comes to gLiTTer...

shoes
headbands
nail polish

enjoy

morE is bEtteR.

Using photos is a wonderful way to add to a story without going into too much detail in the journaling. A picture is truly worth a thousand words, so adding to them is sometimes unnecessary. Nicole's daughter got into crafting with her mom, but her embellishment of choice was glitter. Here, Nicole let the photos do the talking. A close-up of a glitter-covered project and a shot of her daughter's proud face nearly tell the whole story. She wrote a personal commentary, which was just enough to add a little humor and personality.

Supplies: Patterned paper, sticker accents (Scenic Route); chipboard letters (Heidi Swapp); double stick letters (Making Memories); glitter (Martha Stewart); Misc: Typenoksidi font, vintage buttons

Artwork by Nicole Harper

We all have old photos of best friends, birthday parties and school programs. You can write long paragraphs that wax nostalgic or you can make a quick statement to sum it up, as Nicole did here. Like most of us, Nicole had best friends in school with whom she did everything. And then . . . life. She could have gone into detail about what it was like to be so close, and how she wonders about them. Instead, she decided to boil it down to one line, and her brevity is both hilarious and succinct, making the journaling complete.

Supplies: Patterned paper (Anna Griffin, Creative Imaginations); letter stickers (American Crafts); sticker accents (Creative Imaginations, Fontwerks, Heidi Swapp); journal tag (Scenic Route); rub-on (Fontwerks); chipboard accent (Imagination Project); paint (Making Memories); Misc: Times New Roman font, hole punch, staples

Artwork by Nicole Harper

3 summers at band camp.

boyfriends, formal dances and sleepovers.

we swore we'd always be together.

i wonder

I ♥ THE EIGHTIES
1980 1981 1982 1983 1984 1985 1986 1987 1988 1989

REMEMBER

3

★ ★ ★ ★ ★ ★

I wonder where they are now.

still think I don't let you have FUN?

MODERN ROI

1 2 3 4 5 6

GOOD TIMES

fun@

last !!

DREAMS

I pick my battles.
You won this one, Babe.

On this page, I could have gone into detail about how Marc has always wanted to shave his head, but I never let him out of fear that he'd look like a dork. I could have written something about making dreams come true. Or I could have written a nice note about how hot my sweetie ended up looking. But sometimes brevity provides as much meaning— and more personality and authenticity—as several paragraphs. I also chose embellishments that support the page's message. Can't think of your own words? Look to your scrap supplies!

Supplies: Patterned paper (BasicGrey, KI Memories); transparency (Hambly); letter stickers (BasicGrey); embellishments (7gypsies, Making Memories, Scenic Route); rub-on (Imaginisce)

aug. 1999

my favorite

photo

because it brings it all back... how in awe i was of the whole concept of being your mama. and then i see you today...8 years later... i am reminded of just how lucky i am to hold that title. nov. 2007

Artwork by Nicole Harper

Moms, you understand: You could talk for hours about things you love about your child. And long, loving journaling in your scrapbooks is okay. But don't feel like you need to write a novel every time. Nicole loves this photo of her baby girl and wanted to give it special attention. However, instead of rambling on about why she loves the photo, she keeps it short: She simply mentions a few of the feelings that she experiences when she looks at the photo, making the journaling as sweet as the little face on the page.

Supplies: Cardstock; patterned paper (Creative Imaginations, Hambly, Making Memories); felt word (Creative Imaginations); letter sticker, tag (Making Memories); rub-on (Hambly); ribbon (Maya Road); Misc: paint, pen, staples, vintage button

HE IS BRILLIANT.

HE IS COMPASSIONATE.

HE IS HILARIOUS.

HE IS SENSITIVE.

HE IS A DORK.

HE IS PLAYFUL.

HE IS BEAUTIFUL.

HE IS WITTY.

HE IS SWEET.

HE IS OBNOXIOUS.

HE IS LOVING.

HE IS A SPONGE.

HE IS OBLIVIOUS.

HE IS SIX.

HE IS CHALLENGING.

HE IS DISTRACTED.

HE IS GOOFY.

HE IS A NUT.

HE IS A FISHERMAN.

HE IS A TOTAL BOY.

HE IS MY ELDEST.

HE IS A FRIEND.

THIS BOY

and I sure love him.

FOLIO......

TOTAL

NAME......

BOX NUMBERS 1

THE ANTI-PARAGRAPH

Sometimes the very act of writing paragraphs can seem exhausting . . . especially if you're the kind of scrapper who avoids journaling at all costs. But what is a page without your words? Making art is fun, but making a lasting keepsake is even better. So how do you tell your story without having to torture yourself with paragraphs?

Take the pressure off. I'm always making lists—I even have lists of lists that I need to make. If you suffer from this affliction as well, use those lists. Tell future generations what your typical day looks like, what your morning routine is, what you need to get done for the holidays. It's sort of cheating but not really. Even if you write in list form, you are still putting your own words and story on a page.

Question and answer layouts are another easy way to tell a story in authentic voice. You can ask the questions and write down someone's answers in their words. Or even better, use one of the hundreds of personal quizzes and surveys floating around the Internet; all the fun, none of the work! Either way, it's hard to have a Q&A that sounds flat.

So put away the paragraphs. You might be amazed by how much personality comes through in the process!

EVEN IF YOU WRITE A LIST OR USE A Q&A FORMAT, YOU ARE STILL PUTTING YOUR OWN WORDS AND STORY ON A PAGE.

Supplies: Cardstock (Bazzill); patterned paper (Making Memories); border sticker, rub-on (My Mind's Eye); felt (Fancy Pants); foam stickers (American Crafts); label sticker (Scenic Route); Misc: Dad's Recipe font

LISTS

Making a list on a layout may seem like cheating, but it's better than saying nothing. As long as you tell something about yourself (or someone else) on the list, you're sharing your words and your story.

Get connected – Sell your Creativity On-Line.

As designers, we have many outlets for our creativity. We can teach and des... manufacturers, or delve into product development, be published in print perio... the web. There are zines, design teams, on-line pattern companies and ma... websites. We can sell finished projects, kits, or instructions. We can even... an entire book.

Our possibilities are many and growing ev...

Publishing
You can try a self-publishing firm like Lulu.com. This Raleigh, NC-bas... allows you to self–publish your own book or pamphlet. By publishing... (meaning the book isn't printed until the order is placed), the company... thousands of titles on various subjects without limits placed upon the...

At Lulu, you get to price your own book and figure out your own roy... edit, photograph, design and illustrate your entire book, and LULU p... for you. Downside: They do not specifically market to any particula... your work might get lost and is not likely to be picked up by the mass... or the ... But if you are itching to do a book and can't find a publisher to pick up your ideas, this is worth a try! It's ... you have an idea ... costs vary based... The biggest dow... own editor, so if...

Another viable ... projects, kits, or ...

To: My Life
From: Me
Date: October 2006
Re: Notice of my Absence

It's been awhile since we've spoken, but I wanted you to know I will be unavailable for a few weeks.

In the coming month I have to:

* proof and send wedding pix to a bride
* write and edit Designerzine articles
* create layouts for various deadlines
* keep up with the house before seven of my in-laws arrive for Thanksgiving
*feed, clothe, and mother my children
*do all this while Marc hits three states in three weeks

I may go crazy. But you've been warned.

chill

marc's trip sched. —
9th–12th – chicago
24th–27th – milwaukee
5th–9th – san jose

french $!!
for henry!!

10.21.06
DATE TAKEN

This is an actual list I made for myself, and it wasn't so much a "to do" list as it was a reminder of all I had on my plate and how I needed to cut myself some slack. I created this page to mimic a desktop on which I placed my note. It's a jumble of all the things I needed to do, bits of this and that, reminders of things. Sometimes it's a good idea to change it up and create a page as an illustration of the words. Make the page fit the journaling, not the other way around.

Supplies: Cardstock (Bazzill); digital notebook paper (Two Peas in a Bucket); ribbon (Offray); pin (Heidi Grace); acrylic tile (KI Memories); chipboard accent (Scenic Route); sticker accents (7gypsies); pen (Sharpie); Misc: Courier font, buttons

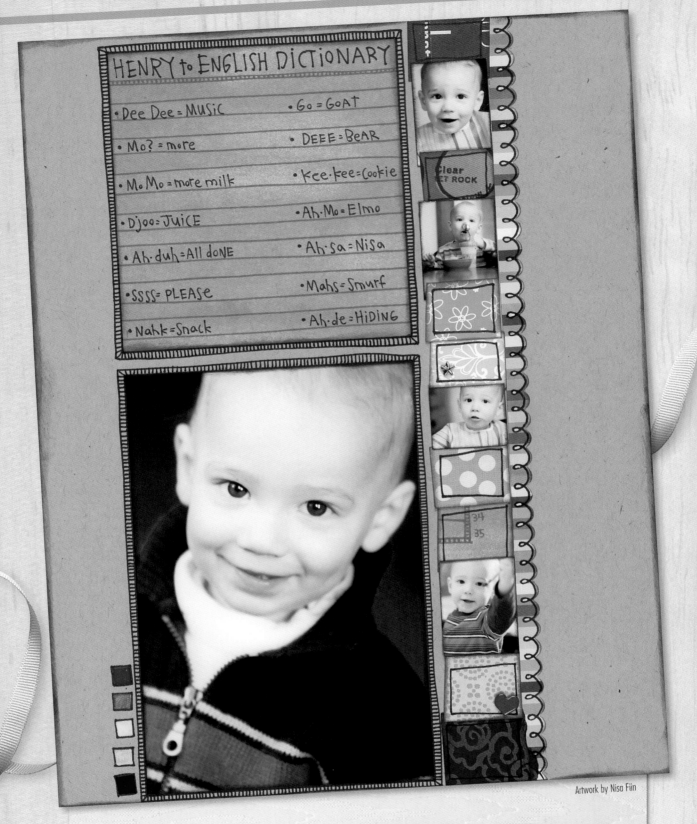

HENRY to ENGLISH DICTIONARY

- Dee Dee = MUSIC
- Mo? = more
- Mo. Mo = more milk
- Djoo = JUICE
- Ah. duh = All DONE
- SSSS = PLEASE
- Nahk = Snack
- Go = GOAT
- DEEE = BeAR
- Kee. kee = Cookie
- Ah. Mo = Elmo
- Ah. sa = Nisa
- Mahs = Smurf
- Ah. de = HiDiNG

clear
ET ROCK

34
35

Artwork by Nisa Fiin

If you have children in your life, you know that they can be an endless source of good journaling. But don't feel like you need to write something pithy or pertinent every time you scrap their silliness. Nisa made a list of Henry's funny ways of saying things. His words and their translations are all that are needed to remind Nisa of how sweet and funny his personality was at that stage of his life.

Supplies: Karft cardstock; patterned paper (7gypsies, American Crafts, Chatterbox, Fontwerks, KI Memories); Misc: brads, pen

If you have only *one photo* *from nearly seven years of your life ...*

From the countless miles swum From the countless practices and meets From countless ribbons and trophies From years of making and breaking personal bests From the summer weekends spent alternately huddling under blankets for warmth and dreading your event, to hiding under tents trying keep your energy from being zapped by the hot sun From USS meets where you cheer on every team member, from the smallest seven-and-unders to the high schoolers you so admire From the high school meets where over the years you get to know the other schools' swimmers and look forward to meets as just another time to say hi From 5 a.m. practices From your team members' parents becoming your own surrogate parents From doing homework by the light of the exit sign at the back of a school bus at 10 p.m. on a school night From way too many McChicken sandwiches and apple pies From spending so much time with the same people that they are pretty much your only pool from which you draw friends and boyfriends From lounging every weekend in the gym of some other school and eating puppy chow, listening to a walkman, playing speed and snuggling in a team parka (even though I never had a team parka and always desperately wanted one) From permanently smelling like chlorine From making it to State ... twice From the local pool to the Notre Dame Natatorium to the Indianapolis Natatorium where the Olympic trials are held From the most significant thing in your life for nearly seven years

make sure it's an amazing **one**

A list doesn't have to start with 1, 2, 3. You can use the same word at the beginning of each line to denote a new statement. And who says there has to be a return after each item? Type your list into a box format, but separate ideas by changing the font color of each one, like I did here. This provides visual flow; it looks like a paragraph, but with a twist. On this page about swimming, I wanted to suggest the look of water, so I made each of the entries a different shade of blue.

Supplies: Cardstock (Bazzill); letter stickers (American Crafts); brads (American Crafts, Queen & Co.); border accent (Doodlebug); Misc: Broadsheet Italic and Century Gothic fonts

OCT 1 2 2007

CONFIDENTIAL

simple things...that let me know you love me.

like putting gas in my car.

or folding the laundry.

or being an amazing Dad to Allie.

simple reasons I love you.

It's all those

funny little ways of yours...

Artwork by Nicole Harper

You may use lists to keep track of what you like or what you do, but how often do you make a list of why you like what you like? Or why you do what you do? Get specific! For example, instead of listing the top ten things you love, take one of those ten—like your husband—and get into the nitty-gritty! Your list can be simple, like Nicole's, or exhaustive. By going into the why of it all, you'll see how even a list can reveal so much of your story.

Supplies: Patterned paper (K&Co., Making Memories); felt trim, sticker accents (Creative Imaginations); vellum file folder (Maya Road); rub-on (Hambly); Misc: Times New Roman font, note card, staples

How you write a list with your journaling is entirely up to you. Sue wrote a few of the issues her daughter faces as she enters her teenage years, creating an informal record of what her daughter's life is like. Jotting down a few thoughts on a topic that follow a singular theme or idea is great for journaling. There's no need to write out entire paragraphs when only a line or two will do.

Supplies: Cardstock, flower (Bazzill); patterned paper (Creative Imaginations); Misc: Verdana font, buttons, floss

Artwork by Sue Thomas

Peer pressure, finding your identity, embarrassed by your parents, mood swings, cliques and ever changing social circles, homework

Struggles at fourteen

QUESTIONS & ANSWERS

With words straight from the horse's mouth, it's hard to have a Q&A that sounds flat. Plus, it provides an easy way to include authentic words on a page.

Why is it that mommies dress their sweet little girls in pink and people STILL ask if Baby is a boy or a girl?

Take Miss Harper here, dressed head-to-tail in pink to play in the leaves. Soon after taking this photo, we ran to the grocery store. At the check-out, the lady behind the register asked,

"Aw! What a cutie! Is it a boy or a girl?"

Um, are you kidding me?

I'm sure it's safer for people to ask than assume, but seriously ... the next time someone asks me this, I am prepared to answer,

It's a **BOY** *but we're hoping for* Gender CONFUSION

As I created this layout about my attitude regarding the question, "Is it a boy or a girl?" I realized the journaling would be more effective and interesting if structured like a question and answer. I created a Q&A on this page by giving special attention to the parts of the journaling that ask and answer the question. You can format Q&A pages however you see fit, depending on the type of page you envision and the voice of the journaling. Remember: The only rules are that you write and use your authentic voice!

Supplies: Cardstock (Bazzill); patterned paper (Creative Imaginations, Heidi Grace); letter stickers (BasicGrey, Doodlebug); chipboard letters (American Crafts, Heidi Swapp); chipboard accents, rub-on stitching (Heidi Grace); border sticker (My Mind's Eye); Misc: Type Slab Serif Light font, ink

- You are almost never late for your appointments
  ✓ YES ○ NO
- You like to be engaged in an active and fast-paced job
  ○ YES ✓ NO
- You enjoy having a wide circle of acquaintances
  ✓ YES ○ NO
- You feel involved when watching TV soaps
  ○ YES ✓ NO
- You are usually the first to react to a sudden event, ie the phone ringing
  ○ YES ✓ NO
- You are more interested in a general idea than in the details of its realization
  ✓ YES ○ NO
- You tend to be unbiased even if this might endanger your good relations with people
  ○ YES ✓ NO
- Strict observance of the established rul[es] likely to prevent a good outcome
  ○ YES ✓ NO
- It's difficult to get you excited
  ○ YES ✓ NO
- It is in your nature to assume responsib[ility]
  ✓ YES ○ NO
- You often think about humankind and destiny
  ✓ YES ○ NO
- You believe the best decision is one th[at] be easily changed
  ○ YES ✓ NO
- Objective criticism is always useful in activity
  ✓ YES ○ NO
- You prefer to act immediately rather th[an] speculate about various options
  ✓ YES ○ NO
- You trust reason rather than feelings
  ✓ YES ○ NO
- You are inclined to rely more on improvisation than on careful planning
  ✓ YES ○ NO
- You spend your leisure time actively socializing with a group of people, attend[ing] parties, shopping, etc.
  ✓ YES ○ NO
- You usually plan your actions in advan[ce]
  ✓ YES ○ NO
- Your actions are frequently influenced [by] emotions
  ✓ YES ○ NO
- You are a person somewhat reserved a[nd] distant in communication
  ✓ YES ○ NO

- You know how to put every minute of your time to good purpose
  ✓ YES ○ NO
- You readily help people while asking nothing in return
  ✓ YES ○ NO
- You often contemplate about the complexity of life
  ✓ YES ○ NO
- After prolonged socializing you feel you need to get away and be alone
  ✓ YES ○ NO
- You often do jobs in a hurry
  ○ YES ✓ NO
- You easily see the general principle behind specific occurrences
  ✓ YES ○ NO
- You frequently and easily express your feelings and emotions
  ✓ YES ○ NO

- You are strongly touched by the stories about people's troubles
  ✓ YES ○ NO
- Deadlines seem to you to be of relative, rather than absolute, importance
  ○ YES ✓ NO
- You prefer to isolate yourself from outside noises
  ○ YES ✓ NO
- It's essential for you to try things with your own hands
  ○ YES ✓ NO
- You think that almost everything can be analyzed
  ○ YES ✓ NO
- You do your best to complete a task on time
  ✓ YES ○ NO
- You take pleasure in putting things in order
  ✓ YES ○ NO

- Your decisions are based more on the feelings of a moment than on the careful planning
  ○ YES ○ NO
- You prefer to spend your leisure time alone or relaxing in a tranquil family atmosphere
  ✓ YES ○ NO
- You feel more comfortable sticking to conventional ways
  ○ YES ○ NO
- You are easily affected by strong emotions
  ✓ YES ○ NO
- You are always looking for opportunities
  ✓ YES ○ NO
- Your desk, workbench etc. is usually neat and orderly
  ○ YES ✓ NO
- As a rule, current preoccupations worry you more than your future plans
  ...leasure from solitary walks
  ○ NO
  ...for you to communicate in social
  ○ NO
  ...nsistent in your habits
  ○ NO
  ...yourself in matters ...thies
  ...ious ways ...elop

The Portait of the Counselor (INFJ)

The Counselor Idealists are abstract in thought and speech, cooperative in reaching their goals, and enterprising and attentive in their interpersonal roles. Counselors focus on human potentials, think in terms of ethical values, and come easily to decisions. The small number of this type (little more than 2 percent) is regrettable, since Counselors have an unusually strong desire to contribute to the welfare of others and genuinely enjoy ...

Your Type is
INFJ

Introverted   Intuitive   Feeling   Judging
Strength of the preferences %

11   38   50   56

When Marc and I were in pre-marital counseling, we took the Myers-Briggs test and I scored as an ENFJ ... much more extrovert than I am now. I was also labeled as the "Consummate Public Relations" type. That worked for me then, as I planned on a career in PR or journalism.
It's funny how being married, living so far from friends and family, and being a stay-home mom for the past eight years has driven the extrovert out of me!
Now I just need to get Marc to take the test again. Back in 1996, he was a to-the-core ISTP, and our counselor told us that Marc's numbers indicated he would not budge an inch on his personality. I wonder if that has held true, or if Marc has shifted over the years, as well!

This is a different take on a Q&A. The questions on the page are from an actual questionnaire, and the answers are my answers. But the journaling itself doesn't really ask or answer anything, it just explains why I included a questionnaire on my layout. Including a Q&A on your layout doesn't exclude you from also writing more journaling. Sometimes it's nice to add to the story. Step outside the journaling block and see all the different possibilities that surround you.

Supplies: Cardstock (Bazzill); patterned paper (Paper Salon); Misc: Century Gothic font, eyelets, floss

PROBLEM SOLVED

"I'm not a typical scrapbooker: I'm single and I don't have kids. I'm the only person who will read my scrapbooks, so why does journaling matter?"

If you're reading this book, you probably feel like you want to say something with your work . . . so journaling does matter. The question is why. Think of your layouts not as a family heirloom, but as a history of what it was like to be you. We find in biographies common threads that tie us all together, regardless of where and when we live. Scrapbooks that you leave behind, no matter where they end up, are your autobiography to share with the world.

Many of my pages speak to what kind of life I live. Take this page: The journaling shares what I've discovered about giving to everyone and everything for too long, and giving nothing to myself along the way. This will be a universal problem for women until the end of time, and if I can stand up and say, "Enough!" maybe someday down the line some other woman will find the strength to say she's had enough, as well.

Times may change, but people do not. And leaving a written record of your life may one day fascinate someone who never knew you in person, and your experience may inspire their life in some way.

Supplies: Cardstock (Bazzill); patterned paper (Collage Press); die-cut paper (KI Memories); letter stickers (Doodlebug); rub-on letters (American Crafts); graphic rub-on (7gypsies); label stickers (Jenni Bowlin); Misc: Book Antiqua font

Unanswered Questions

How did you meet?

What attracted you to each other?

How long did you date?

How did he propose?

When were you married?

What did your ring look like?

Did you have a honeymoon?

Did you talk about having a baby?

Were you friends?

Do you have happy memories?

What were we like as a family?

When did you know it wouldn't last?

Was your heart broken?

These are questions I'll likely never ask.

Probably because I know I won't get answers.

Is there something in your life that you question daily? Have you ever considered writing those questions on a layout? You may not have answers, but some dynamic writing can come from getting those big questions on paper. This layout came about after I found these old photos of my parents before their divorce, and I realized I had no idea who these people were. That I have no answers to go with my questions is, in fact, the answer I had to write on the page.

Supplies: Cardstock (Bazzill); patterned paper (My Mind's Eye); letter stickers (BasicGrey); die-cut tag (K&Co.); rub-ons (7gypsies, October Afternoon); Misc: Californian font

Ironic...

(Actual conversation ... more or less ... that took place between Marc and Michele on a summer weekend in 1999, while visiting Indiana. There was lots of time to talk in the car.)

That this was the weekend we got pregnant with Henry.

Question #1:
Michele – "Do you think we need to talk about when we want to start a family?"
Marc – "Why? When we're ready, we'll know."

Question #2:
Michele – "That's just it. When will we know we're ready?"
Marc – "Who knows. We just will."

Question #3:
Michele – "Okay. So, like, next year?"
Marc – "Yeah. Next year. We'll see if we're ready to talk about it in a year."
Michele – "Okay. One year gives me time to figure out what I want to do."

The Q&A journaling on this layout consists of a conversation between me and Marc many years ago. If a conversation leads to something significant, make sure you write what was asked and what was answered! Have you made a big decision that required a lot of questioning? Do you frequently argue over little things that no one will decide? Do you often ask for more information or more explanation? Keep an ear open to all the possible Q&As you can write about.

Supplies: Cardstock (Bazzill); patterned paper (American Crafts, BasicGrey, Chatterbox); letter stickers (BasicGrey); border punch (EK Success); Misc: Muriel, Times New Roman and Tradition Sans Light fonts

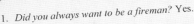

Q&A WITH DAD

1. *Did you always want to be a fireman?* Yes.

2. *Did you ever get to ride on the back of a truck?* Yes. You mean like the old guys? Yes.

3. *What's more fun: holding the hoses or going into the building?* Going in.

4. *How many lives did you save?* Millions. (Ha.) That's hard to say. As a fireman or as a medic? You like to think you helped save a handful. I saved cats. And dogs.

5. *Were you ever scared?* Probably. But it's like a calculated risk. If you know what you need to know, there's no reason to go in if it's too bad. There's no reason to be scared if you know what to expect.

6. *Why did you go to art school?* Because everybody thought I should. I was a doodler, and people thought I should go to art school. I had a great time, and if I hadn't gone you wouldn't be here. But I really wanted to be a fireman.

7. *Did you think of yourself as a hero or was it just a job?* There has to be a certain amount of ego in a job like a cop or a fireman, but I never thought of myself as a hero. I was just grateful to do a job that mattered.

8. *Was being a fireman a "cool" job, or is that just a post-9.11 thing?* Oh, it was a cool job. There were never two days alike.

9. *If I'd had a Career day at school when I was a kid, would you have come in to talk about being a fireman?* Certainly.

10. *Would you have worn your gear?* Yes. I would have brought it, and I would have let you wear it.

11. *Do you miss it?* I did. By the time I had 20 years in, I'd been a white shirt for 10 years. I missed fire fighting when I went into the office, but by the time I retired, I didn't miss it anymore.

12. *Is it in the contract that firemen have to have a mustache?* Nope. But no beards allowed.

13. *Was it a way to have the brothers that you didn't have growing up?* Yeah, kind of. You're really close to the guys you work with because you spend more time with them then you do with your family. Plus you have to trust them with your life.

14. *Should I switch careers and give it a whirl?* It's something you don't just decide to do. A lot have thought about giving it a try, but fire fighting is a predestined thing. If you don't have a love for it, you're not going to be safe.

15. *What type of truck was your favorite to drive?* Engine. You got to operate all the dials and controls. Or maybe the ladder truck … they're cool.

16. *Did you ever climb all the way up on a ladder truck?* Oh yeah. 100 feet up. It's like a free ride on a Ferris wheel.

17. *What kind of life insurance can you get when you're in that line of work?* Hmm … never thought about it. I had life insurance, so I guess it didn't matter that I was a fireman.

18. *Who was the best cook?* Everybody was pretty good. I was pretty good. They're all good out of necessity.

19. *Did you ever have a Dalmatian?* No.

Of course, using an actual Q&A session is a wonderful way to get authentic voices on a page—not only your own, but also someone else's. I realized one night that in all my 34 years, I'd never really asked my dad about his job as a fireman. So I held a mini interview. Is there someone you wish you knew better? Write questions and give that person a call. If you fear the response, make sure to keep your questions lighthearted. You'll still come away with great journaling.

Supplies: Cardstock (Bazzill); patterned paper (Pebbles); chipboard letters (Cosmo Cricket); letter stickers (American Crafts); Misc: Times New Roman font

to do
BEFORE i die

{in no particular order...}

1. Lose 50 pounds.

2. Speak another language fluently. Preferably Spanish or French.

3. Learn to play the guitar.

4. Watch the July 4th fireworks from an airplane.

5. Have a truly romantic moment. Preferably with Marc.

6. Go somewhere amazing for a location photography class.

7. Swim the Mile Meet.

8. Take the kids to the Galápagos and Ecuador to show them where Marc was born and raised.

9. Chase tornados.

10. Know that I raised my kids to be good, giving, loving, respectful, polite and intelligent people.

11. Figure out what I want to be when I grow up.

12. Travel to Ireland. And England. And Prague, Greece, Italy, Brittany, New Zealand, Estonia, Finland, Costa Rica, Belize, Spain, Morocco, Patagonia, Sweden, Switzerland, Cabo, Bhutan, Tibet, Norway, and live on a sailboat somewhere tropical for no less than a week. And then onto the places in the U.S. ...

13. Have the guts to have a real conversation with my parents about their life and relationship before me.

14. Be at peace within myself.

15. Retire to a place where Marc and I can sit on Adirondack chairs in our yard and watch the water on the lake or ocean.

16. Preferably in New England.

GRAND TOTAL,

TERMINAL AUDIENCE

We are all given this opportunity called Life. Some of us are even lucky enough to pass it on to children. Regardless of how we spend it and how long we have it, life is a gift, and one we should cherish.

How does this fit in with writing? Well, truth is, none of us know how long we have on this planet. We feel invincible and are living under the presumption that we and our loved ones will be around for so long that it doesn't matter whether we say what's in our hearts; there is always tomorrow. Well, for the sake of good journaling, let's say life doesn't last forever. And let's say that we're given this opportunity to scrapbook as a way to share what's in our hearts with those who mean the most to us.

As Annie Dillard wrote in her book, *A Writer's Life*:

"Write as if you were dying. At the same time, assume you write for an audience consisting solely of terminal patients. That is, after all, the case. What would you begin writing if you knew you would die soon? What could you say to a dying person that would not enrage by its triviality?"

That Annie is a smart cookie.

If you had the chance to truly share your heart with your partner, your child, your parents, your friends, what would you say? Will you say something trivial, as Annie puts it, or will you stretch your neck and take a risk and really say what you want them to hear? This is probably one of the hardest challenges to writing, especially in a scrapbook. The fear of really putting yourself out there and opening yourself up to criticism is just plain scary. But to truly reveal yourself, even if you're just writing down your hopes and fears and thoughts for your own eyes, write it like you'll never get another chance to say it. You won't regret it.

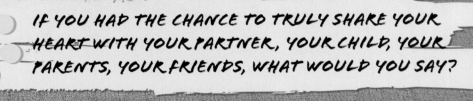

IF YOU HAD THE CHANCE TO TRULY SHARE YOUR HEART WITH YOUR PARTNER, YOUR CHILD, YOUR PARENTS, YOUR FRIENDS, WHAT WOULD YOU SAY?

Supplies: Cardstock (Bazzill); patterned paper (Heidi Grace, Making Memories); letter stickers (American Crafts); chipboard letters (Heidi Swapp); photo corners (Making Memories); stamp (7gypsies); scallop punch (Marvy); dimensional paint (Ranger); Misc: Apple Garamond Light font

ABOUT ME AND YOU AND LIFE

There's no one right way to share your heart with an audience. You can address someone directly, share your perspective, or just muse for a while, just as long as you write without fear.

know you

Do you know what scares me? One inevitable day you'll come to me, asking how to know who you are, and I won't have answers for you. After 34 years, I'm just now realizing that I myself have no idea who I am. And how can I teach you to be true to yourself when I feel like my whole life has been a lie?

After a disjointed childhood full of never belonging, never being "right," never having a solid foundation, after living with years of emotional abuse and always being the outsider, I learned that being "me" was a problem. The easier way to navigate life was to be what "they" wanted – whoever "they" were at the time.

I bounced around from friend to friend, job to job, hobby to hobby, always looking for a "fit," always wanting to "fit in." And just when I'd get close, I'd do something to screw up, or the act of fitting in would get too hard and I'd drop out, regroup, and reinvent myself. I think I got used to my family moving every two years because then I could reinvent who I was based on what was required to make friends and survive in my new environment.

In many ways, I was relieved to have you. I could just be Mom, and I could find an easy identity in that. And the thought of quitting my job to stay home with you filled me with relief. I had become so good at not attaching myself to things, not applying myself, not giving a damn, that working wasn't very fun, regardless of the job. But being a mom presented a whole new set of issues. Bigger ones. Because now I had to be the example; the one instilling my child with a sense of value and self-worth, and that's a tall order for someone who feels no value and self-worth. The good thing is that you are a phenomenal child and there's hope that you'll be just fine.

I strive to give you confidence and stability so that you can figure out who you are and where you're going in life, but who knows if that's what it takes. Maybe by trying to make sure I don't screw you up, I'll inadvertently do the opposite. I just want you to be happy, but how can you find your way in this world if I'm constantly trying to steer you down a clear path? I get it, really … life happens, and who we are depends on how we respond to it. Okay.

Know **THYSELF** *Socrates*

Honestly, Henry, I'll probably learn more about who I am by letting you live your own life and watching you be your own navigator.

This page about, and for, my son also reveals a lot about me. Right now, my son is too young to care what I write in his scrapbooks. But as he grows older, with any luck, it will help him understand where I'm coming from and know that I've been where he's going. And maybe he'll learn from me. If your journaling can somehow make sense of something, or can relate your perspective to why you do and say certain things, your words, no matter who they are for, will tell your story.

Supplies: Patterned paper (Collage Press, K&Co.); chipboard letters (Heidi Grace); chipboard accents (K&Co.); scallop label (Jenni Bowlin); bracket stickers (Doodlebug); rub-on (7gypsies); date paper (Knock Knock); Misc: Times New Roman font

Sometimes I think, "what if I die young?"

Will they remember that my favorite color is yellow or that I have to sleep with socks on no matter what the temperature is? Will Cassandra remember the summer we watched the entire series of Star Trek Voyager because we're both geeks? Will Ian remember our special roars when we raid the fridge for cheese sticks? How about the many nights I spent breastfeeding them and rocking them to sleep? The silly songs I made up with their nicknames? And the many messes we made creating stuff? The summers we spent cuddling in the hammock and watching the sunset?

There are so many things I have yet to teach them. So many things I want them to remember about me, about the things we've done together. I want to watch them grow and see what happens. I want to be surprised, excited, happy and, at times, scared and frustrated for them.

But, most of all, I just want to love them and never ever let go.

[thoughts]

Artwork by Sandra Stephens

One common mistake we make is to leave ourselves out of the story. We rarely have photos of ourselves because we're always the one holding the camera. We share our perspective on memories, but we don't put much of ourselves on the page. We create books so our children will have a record of their lives and how we feel about them, but what about recording our lives too? I challenge you to create a page like Sandra's. From the simple and silly details about you, to the more introspective aspects, write it down!

Supplies: Patterned paper (Daisy D's); journaling paper, lace, tag (Making Memories); rub-on word (Urban Lily); flower (My Mind's Eye); lace paper (KI Memories)

Is there someone in your life who always brings you happiness and comfort, who is always there for you? Tell them how you feel! We tend to learn too late that we should tell the people we love how we feel about them, and thank them for what they've brought to our life. Right now, think of someone who holds a special place in your heart, and write down exactly what they have given to you. Whether you share the journaling with them is up to you.

Supplies: Patterned paper (7gypsies, Making Memories, Scenic Route); letter stickers (Scenic Route); brads, rub-on letters (American Crafts); decorative tape (7gypsies); sticker accents (Creative Imaginations, KI Memories); rub-on accent (Hambly); stamp (Jenni Bowlin); Misc: ink, pen, staples

Artwork by Nicole Harper

while i'm thinking about it...

i want you to know... i look up to you - you have made me who i am today. while you may not think so, i think you're incredibly strong. you're an amazing woman... know that. the greatest gift you've ever given me is being a grandma to Allie. your laugh is completely contagious. i love that we have our own 'language.' you're my favorite travel partner... even when the road gets rough. and about a million other things, Mom... so much to say... so much...

FIND BALANCE   FIND BALANCE
I adore you (always will).

i sHoulD tell you

Training A lifetime pursuit

You have been an avid cyclist for the majority of my life. Daily rides either as transportation to and from the bike shop you owned or on the rollers in the basement if the weather was bad, weekend road races, cyclists dropping in at our house, and the smell of wet wool drying in the laundry room were all regular parts of my childhood. I've been out of the house for a "few" years now and yet the memories come flooding back when I see your jersey hanging on your closet door - evidence of continued pursuit of your training.

Artwork by Sue Thomas

You can go about addressing someone in your journaling in different ways. You can go deep and pour your heart out, or you can choose one aspect of that person, reflect on it and make it special. That is what Sue did with the journaling about her father's commitment to cycling. She brings out her own sensory memories as a way to pay tribute to her father's passion. Like Sue, you can't speak for someone else, but you can use your own memories to create a picture of a part of that person's life.

Supplies: Cardstock; patterned paper (Autumn Leaves)

up here

35,000 feet above ground, and I feel at peace. There's something about flying that equals serenity for me. It's the only place that I feel like I can really relax. Perhaps it's because there's so much that I simply can't do in the air. I play taxi for the kids, unload the dishwasher, pick up mess in the mudroom, start a load of laundry. I don't have to feel guilty for listening to my ipod & reading a book. Or sketching out scrapbooking ideas. Or even just letting my mind wander. There's a sense of anonymity in the air...I don't have to be a mom, a wife, a sister, a daughter...I'm just Seat 14B. The hassles of travel & the chaos of everyday life melt away as the plane climbs higher. It must be the air up here.

Artwork by Katrina Simeck

Most people wouldn't consider an airplane a retreat, but for Katrina, it's just that. She loves that during a flight she can focus on herself, do what she wants and bask in her own little space in which she can just be. Is there a particular place that is just for you, where you get your "me" time? Is there a place where you don't have to wear all the hats that define you? Write about that place. Put down on paper what it is that makes it such a free zone.

Supplies: Cardstock; patterned paper (Scenic Route); letter stickers (American Crafts); brads (Stemma)

ABOUT HOPES AND FEARS

Hopes and fears are the best and the worst parts of our deepest hearts. So what better things to share with a "terminal" audience than these?

I know you want to fly. It's your one greatest dream. And you know I hate when you fly. It's my one greatest fear. But have I really driven you to going up in little planes on the down-low? Behind my back? How little respect do you have for my fear? Then again, how little respect do I have for your one true love ...? Hmm. Sorry.

What part of

"over my cold dead body!"

do you not understand??

hope it was worth it!! ☺

When I found these photos, I had to construct a page to voice my fear and frustration over my husband's flying. As I wrote about my frustration that he wasn't respecting my fear, I began to realize that he was probably frustrated with me for not respecting his dream. See? The act of authentic writing can bring you to a place of resolution. What is your fear? Write it down. As the words form on the page, you may find yourself seeing it in a different light.

Supplies: Cardstock (Bazzill); patterned paper (BasicGrey, Piggy Tales); chipboard mats (Die Cuts With A View); chipboard buttons (KI Memories); Misc: 2 Peas Jack Frost and Century Gothic fonts, floss

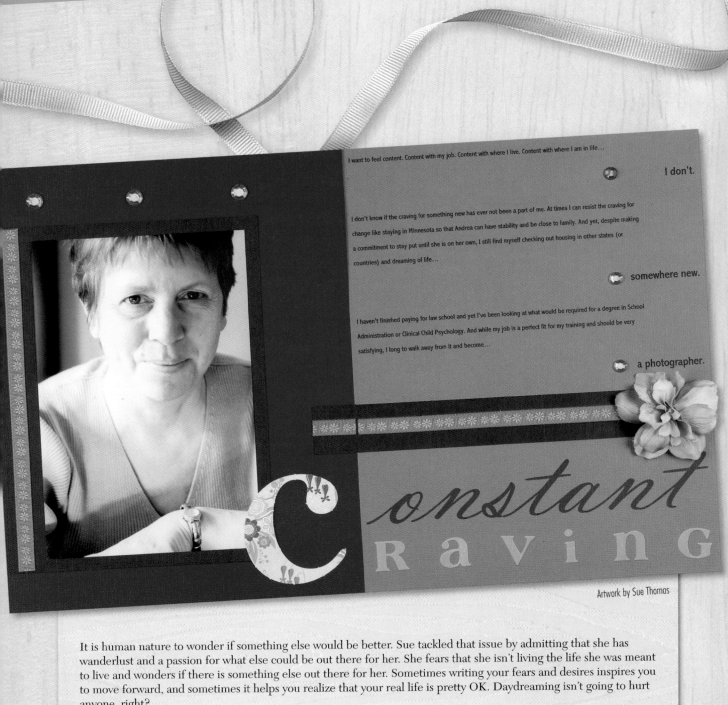

I want to feel content. Content with my job. Content with where I live. Content with where I am in life...

I don't.

I don't know if the craving for something new has ever not been a part of me. At times I can resist the craving for change like staying in Minnesota so that Andrea can have stability and be close to family. And yet, despite making a commitment to stay put until she is on her own, I still find myself checking out housing in other states (or countries) and dreaming of life...

somewhere new.

I haven't finished paying for law school and yet I've been looking at what would be required for a degree in School Administration or Clinical Child Psychology. And while my job is a perfect fit for my training and should be very satisfying, I long to walk away from it and become...

a photographer.

Constant Craving

Artwork by Sue Thomas

It is human nature to wonder if something else would be better. Sue tackled that issue by admitting that she has wanderlust and a passion for what else could be out there for her. She fears that she isn't living the life she was meant to live and wonders if there is something else out there for her. Sometimes writing your fears and desires inspires you to move forward, and sometimes it helps you realize that your real life is pretty OK. Daydreaming isn't going to hurt anyone, right?

Supplies: Cardstock; large monogram, letter stickers (BasicGrey); rhinestones (Target); flower (Jo-Ann); ribbon (American Crafts); Misc: Abadi MT and AL Aunt Marie fonts

PROBLEM SOLVED

"All I scrap about are my pets and my travels. Emotional journaling doesn't fit my photos. How can I write anything personal on those pages?"

Even if you only take nature photos or shots of your pets, there's no rule that says you have to write just the facts. You can look at your photos and try to find something personal in them. Does a place awaken an energy or spirituality in you? Does your pet make you laugh or remind you of your childhood? Does the process of taking macro shots of flowers drive you crazy? Take the time to see your photos from a different point of view.

I spent a few days in Saugatuck, Michigan, and was so inspired by the place. It truly was a town that could become "home", and instantly I was filled with ideas of what Marc and I could do if we lived there and what our quality of life might be like. So instead of just putting beautiful photographs on a page and titling it, "Saugatuck," I also added a small spot of journaling that reveals my daydreams about living there.

Impersonal photos can elicit personal thoughts. Whether you are able to write paragraphs or just jot down a few ideas, you are still finding yourself and your story.

Supplies: Cardstock (Bazzill); patterned paper (Scenic Route); tags (Collage Press); rub-on (Heidi Swapp); die-cut accent (Pebbles); flowers (Prima); paper border (Doodlebug); Misc: Bix Antique Script font, pen

What if you followed your heart and entered the military after high school?
What if you became a fighter pilot or sniper, like you wanted?
What if you became a fighter pilot or sniper, like you wanted?
What if your mom hadn't told you to try a year of college first?
What if that year of college hadn't fueled your passion for computers?
What if that year of college hadn't changed the course of education?
What if you hadn't chosen to stay the course of education?
What if things were different?

We never would have met.
We never would have had our kids.
We never would have built this life together.

I shudder to think.

About the **what ifs**

Do you ever wonder what life would be like had you not made a certain decision? We all live with the "what ifs" in our heads, but have you ever written about them? My husband had a whole different life planned for himself, and I know that my life would be completely changed if he had gone down his own path. Make a page and write about your "what ifs," your fears for the future, how making a decision may or may not change the course of your life.

Supplies: Patterned paper (BasicGrey, Collage Press); letter stickers (American Crafts); border sticker, tags (Collage Press); label holder, paper clip (Making Memories); word sticker (7gypsies); Misc: Splendid 66 font

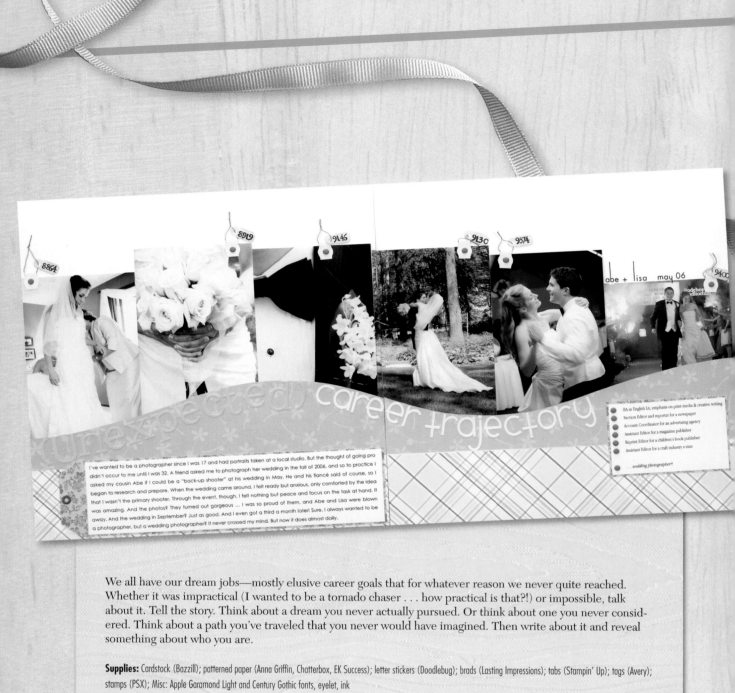

unexpected career trajectory

8864 8919 9146 9130 9374 9400

abe + lisa may 06

- BA in English Lit, emphasis on print media & creative writing
- Section Editor and reporter for a newspaper
- Account Coordinator for an advertising agency
- Assistant Editor for a magazine publisher
- Reprint Editor for a children's book publisher
- Assistant Editor for a craft industry e-zine

. . . wedding photographer!?

I've wanted to be a photographer since I was 17 and had portraits taken at a local studio. But the thought of going pro didn't occur to me until I was 32. A friend asked me to photograph her wedding in the fall of 2006, and so to practice I asked my cousin Abe if I could be a "back-up shooter" at his wedding in May. He and his fiancé said of course, so I began to research and prepare. When the wedding came around, I felt ready but anxious, only comforted by the idea that I wasn't the primary shooter. Through the event, though, I felt nothing but peace and focus on the task at hand. It was amazing. And the photos? They turned out gorgeous ... I was so proud of them, and Abe and Lisa were blown away. And the wedding in September? Just as good. And I even got a third a month later! Sure, I always wanted to be a photographer, but a wedding photographer? It never crossed my mind. But now it does almost daily.

We all have our dream jobs—mostly elusive career goals that for whatever reason we never quite reached. Whether it was impractical (I wanted to be a tornado chaser . . . how practical is that?!) or impossible, talk about it. Tell the story. Think about a dream you never actually pursued. Or think about one you never considered. Think about a path you've traveled that you never would have imagined. Then write about it and reveal something about who you are.

Supplies: Cardstock (Bazzill); patterned paper (Anna Griffin, Chatterbox, EK Success); letter stickers (Doodlebug); brads (Lasting Impressions); tabs (Stampin' Up); tags (Avery); stamps (PSX); Misc: Apple Garamond Light and Century Gothic fonts, eyelet, ink

It's a secret so you have to promise that you won't tell a sole. My high school is filled with hOTTies! They are everywhere! At the next locker, all over the halls, in my classes and even sharing a stand with me in orchestra! I'm going to love high school!!!! Shh…

shh...

Artwork by Sue Thomas

The secrets of children are generally sweet and innocent. Have you ever thought of writing them down? In the not-so-distant future, the kids in your life will probably stop confiding their deepest thoughts in you, so it might be nice to preserve this fleeting aspect of your relationship. Recording a child's secret, like Sue did, also serves another purpose: It will show them, years down the road, the progression of what was important to them. They will laugh or roll their eyes over what they thought was top secret, and will hopefully be grateful for the reminder of a simpler time.

Supplies: Cardstock; patterned paper (My Mind's Eye); chipboard letters (All My Memories, Heidi Swapp, Scenic Route); rub-on (BasicGrey); brads (Making Memories); Misc: 2 Peas Busy Bobs and Zapfellipt fonts, ink, spray paint

HAIKU: Entitled { Cooperation as seen in marriage }

Ugh. There's that camera.

You just keep shooting, honey.

Tonight: Halo 3

GENRE

Sometimes a layout requires a little more creativity and fun than usual. You can play with words and explore all manners of genre—even fiction and poetry—and yet still retain your authentic voice and personality.

Think back to the writing assignments your teachers gave you in school. You probably wrote a poem or two about a memory or special object. Then there are those fairytales you wrote when you were a kid. Have you ever spent hours coming up with the 17 simple syllables that would create a poignant or hilarious haiku? Try including these genres in your scrapbooks. Doing so gives you greater freedom to explore emotion without getting too personal, and it helps you avoid getting bogged down by details. And it gives you a place to spread your wings and let your words and your story take flight.

Writing in different genres also allows you to use photos you might otherwise overlook. Maybe you have a not-so-great photo of an important memory. Liven up the photo with some creativity! Or maybe you have a great shot, but there isn't anything to write beyond the thousand words the photo itself provides. So write a limerick or a haiku, anything that gives the page a little kick. Use your photos to illustrate a whole new story!

Let your inner creative writer out to play on occasion and see what she has to offer. You might be surprised how easy it is to write when you take away the pressure.

WRITING IN DIFFERENT GENRES GIVES YOU FREEDOM TO EXPLORE EMOTION WITHOUT GETTING TOO PERSONAL, AND IT HELPS YOU AVOID GETTING BOGGED DOWN BY DETAILS.

Supplies: Cardstock (Bazzill); patterned paper (7gypsies, BasicGrey, Scenic Route); die-cut letters (QuicKutz); buttons (SE!); brackets (American Crafts); Misc: Times New Roman font

FICTION

Whether it's a limerick, fairytale or haiku, fiction gives any page a little kick. And it gives you the freedom you need to let go of your writing inhibitions.

Once Upon a Time

joy

... in a land not so far away, there lived a beautiful little girl. This little girl had a wonderful life, filled with playing with her older brother and wearing his hand-me-downs, running around outside and digging in the dirt, and obsessing over ladybugs and moths. She was a happy little girl and didn't feel there was anything missing from her life.

Then one day she went to the home of another little girl, and a whole new world appeared. She discovered dress-up clothes, jewelry and crowns, play kitchens and baby dolls. And this little girl's eyes grew wide and her smile grew broad across her sweet little face, which was adorned with a Bob the Builder bandage on her cheek.

Her mother saw the little girl's curiosity and joy, and vowed that day to bring more girly things into the home.

The very next day, a journey was made to the magical boutique known around the land as Target, home of all your heart's desires. The little girl and her mom went up and down the aisles until they saw it: the reason for their journey. A lavender and pink gossamer gown, covered with lace and glittery things. And what's more, there was a hat. And on the very next shelf, shoes and a matching wand.

Smiles and giggles were heard throughout the land as the little girl and her mother returned to their home and the gown was placed upon the girl's body. Instantly, a princess was born. And she grew stronger and more lovely every day. Though she still loved to dig in the dirt. Especially if she was wearing pink.

THE END

If you look through your photos, I guarantee that you'll find several you can easily write about if you start with the words "Once upon a time . . ." Give it a try! "Once upon a time, a boy met a girl." "Once upon a time, you had hair." "Once upon a time, my life was so very different." You can go anywhere with those four little words. Of course, if you have photos of a princess, writing a fairytale is a given.

Supplies: Cardstock (Bazzill); patterned paper (Crafter's Workshop, Paper Salon); letter stickers (Making Memories); chipboard accents (Jenni Bowlin, Making Memories, Sonburn, Technique Tuesday); ribbon (KI Memories); epoxy sticker (Stemma); rhinestones (Heidi Swapp); stamps (Autumn Leaves); Misc: CAC One Seventy font, ink, paint

Haiku for Photography:

Every day I take | photographs of the small stuff | that makes art of life.

Just because a scrapbook page features beautiful photography that speaks all on its own doesn't mean it has to be devoid of your voice. Even if you have nothing profound to say, put your touch on it somewhere. A haiku is a lovely choice. With three lines of five, seven and five syllables, it's easier than writing a poem and less stressful than actual journaling. It doesn't have to be emotional or pertinent. All it has to do is lend a little "you" to the page.

Supplies: Cardstock (Bazzill); digital frame by Katie Pertiet (Designer Digitals); Misc: Apple Garamond Light font

You can create a whole album full of layouts with little haikus for journaling. They say so much in their few words and can inform just as easily as they entertain or inspire. Catherine chose to spend her 17 syllables on telling her kids that she loves them. It's nothing grandiose or time-consuming, but still so sweet and honest. Even in specific writing genres, there are no rules. How you choose to approach it is entirely up to you.

Supplies: Patterned paper (A2Z, Scenic Route); transparency (Hambly); stamps (7gypsies, Heidi Swapp); tab, tag (Avery); Misc: ink, paint

Artwork by Catherine Feegel-Erhardt

Her name was supposed to be "Annabelle."

But it would have been too expensive to spell.

The letter stickers her mom would need –

Two A_s, N_s, L_s, and E_s –

Would have caused the cost of scrapping to swell.

Limerick

harper lillian, NOT annabelle mae

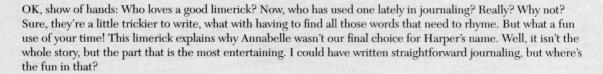

OK, show of hands: Who loves a good limerick? Now, who has used one lately in journaling? Really? Why not? Sure, they're a little trickier to write, what with having to find all those words that need to rhyme. But what a fun use of your time! This limerick explains why Annabelle wasn't our final choice for Harper's name. Well, it isn't the whole story, but the part that is the most entertaining. I could have written straightforward journaling, but where's the fun in that?

Supplies: Cardstock (Bazzill); patterned paper (Sassafras Lass); rub-on letters (American Crafts); brads (Karen Foster); ribbons (KI Memories, Making Memories); Misc: Temps Nouveau and Wendy Medium fonts

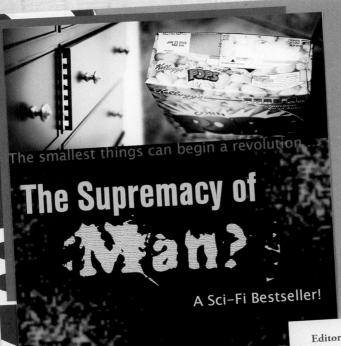

The smallest things can begin a revolution...

The Supremacy of Man?

A Sci-Fi Bestseller!

SCIENCE FICTION
or WiSHfUl tHiNkiNg?

Editorial Review:

It is the year 2045, and the minds of science have finally cracked genetic engineering to create a perfect species. Their objective: to create the genetically perfect Man. The world has spiraled out of control with wars, global warming, and the near-apocalyptic Battle of the Sexes. Men have been reduced to Lawn Keepers, Bug Killers and Reachers of Stuff on the High Shelf by the uprising Woman class, who finally reached the end of their collective ropes. Driven by necessity and frustration and fear of extinction, the Woman class has evolved into a super-human race, with brains more brilliant and bodies more capable of doing it all. But now the race is nearing exhaustion and realizing that the Man is truly needed. The genetically altered Man is exceptional; he is thoughtful, compassionate, has no interest in the remote control or the Military Channel, and is capable of astounding feats of opening the cereal box and bag correctly, managing to get clothes into the laundry chute, and closing dresser drawers all the way. Every single time.

But will this new, perfect race be the solution to the problem? What new struggles will arise? Will the Woman class once again fall into submission? And just who will win the fight for dominancy as Supreme Flying Car-Driving Captain?

In this thought-provoking book, science fiction has never seemed so timely ... or providential.

a girl can dream, right?

When I say, "play with genres," I mean it! Anything you can think of writing, write! Describe your wedding rehearsal as a horror story. Tell the story of how you met your spouse as a romance novel. Write about a vacation like it's an action-adventure script. When I walk through the house and see all the little signs that Marc has been there, I have to laugh. How many times do I have to ask, "Is it really so hard to close the drawers all the way?" Then it hit me: Here are the makings of the perfect sci-fi book!

Supplies: Cardstock (Bazzill, WorldWin); patterned paper (KI Memories); chipboard and rub-on letters (American Crafts); letter stickers (Doodlebug); tag (Chatterbox); rub-on accents (7gypsies); Misc: Apple Garamond Pro, Basketcase, Lucida San and Nimbus San fonts

NON-FICTION

Non-fiction doesn't mean boring or stodgy; you can still let your creativity loose. Try a want ad, a guide book, or a "harrowing true story" to keep your layouts engaging and fresh.

It drew you to it from the moment Greg hung it from the tree in the front yard. You would master the secret hidden in the knots of it's clean white surface. With this secret, you would master the new challenge that called to you each time you walked past the picture window in the living room. You would become the master of... THE ROPE!

You spent an entire weekend determined to get up that rope. You changed gloves, you changed techniques, you asked for tips from Greg and me and each of your friends that came by. You jumped, you pulled, you hung, but you could not get up that rope. Your efforts were obvious in the trampled snow under the rope. Evidence that despite the setbacks, you did not give up. I would love to report that because of your hard work, you were able to get up the rope and touch the branch of the tree but in reality, you have decided that for now, swinging from the rope with Otis running back and forth after your feet is just as rewarding as making it up the rope.

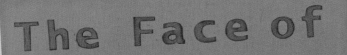

The Face of Determination

Artwork by Sue Thomas

Any writing teacher will tell you that to write a good plot, a protagonist must have an antagonist. In other words, to have a fully formed story, you need to explain why your subject does what he does. Sue's description of her daughter's determination to climb a rope would be a nice observation of Andrea's personality on its own, but turning the rope into a character gives power to Andrea's perseverance. This layout shows that you can tell a creative story with your journaling without having to generate a work of fiction.

Supplies: Cardstock; patterned paper, sticker accent (Creative Imaginations); Misc: AL Clean Lines font, ink

PROBLEM SOLVED

"My biggest problem is coming up with titles.
Are there any secrets to that?"

Titles are definitely tricky. There are times when I leave one off altogether because there just isn't anything good to call a page. Other times, a title is completely unnecessary.

One route to go when looking for a title is to take words directly from your journaling. Either repeat them as the title or set them apart from the journaling by bolding the letters, using a new font or putting them in their own space. Quotes and lyrics also make great titles. How you write is also another thing to consider. When I see a photo, almost instantly a snarky or silly or sweet caption pops into my head. Many times, I end up using that as a title for a subsequent page that features the photo or photos. If you are stumped, look to pre-made titles. However, don't feel like you need to leave it as is. You can personalize store-bought titles by adding another word or two with complementary supplies.

On this layout, I could have gone with something simple like "Fortunes," but I wanted to hint at the funny story I tell in the journaling. Plus, I wanted to balance the actual fortunes with title strips, requiring more words than one.

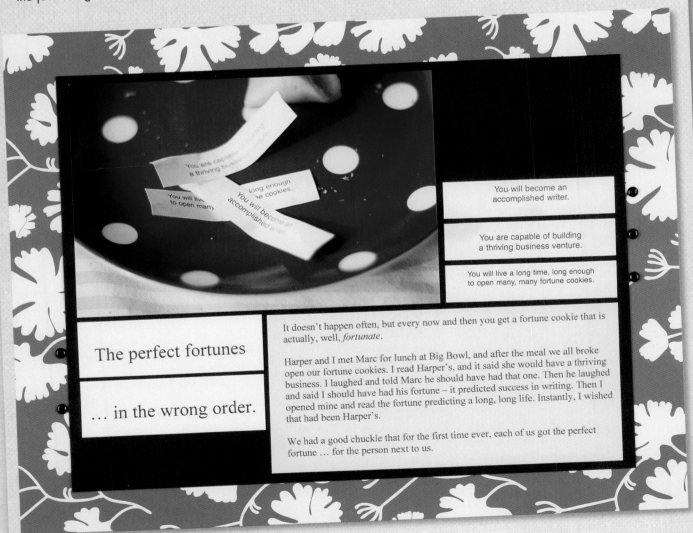

You will become an accomplished writer.

You are capable of building a thriving business venture.

You will live a long time, long enough to open many, many fortune cookies.

The perfect fortunes

... in the wrong order.

It doesn't happen often, but every now and then you get a fortune cookie that is actually, well, *fortunate*.

Harper and I met Marc for lunch at Big Bowl, and after the meal we all broke open our fortune cookies. I read Harper's, and it said she would have a thriving business. I laughed and told Marc he should have had that one. Then he laughed and said I should have had his fortune – it predicted success in writing. Then I opened mine and read the fortune predicting a long, long life. Instantly, I wished that had been Harper's.

We had a good chuckle that for the first time ever, each of us got the perfect fortune … for the person next to us.

Supplies: Cardstock (Bazzill); patterned paper (American Crafts); brads (Making Memories); Misc: Times New Roman font

help wanted.

LAUNDRY PERSON

Must be able to process multiple loads of laundry in an efficient manner. Needs to be able to predict which pair of jeans will be desperately needed on any given day. Experience with getting grass stains out of sports uniforms and white socks desired.

TAXI DRIVER

Must be able to make multiple trips to the same destination on the same day without expressing frustration. Should be familiar with all sports schedules, as well as the location of all area recreational fields. Tolerance for loud music required.

SHORT ORDER COOK

Must be able to provide three balanced meals per day, plus multiple snacks. Ability to brew a good pot of coffee is essential. Will be required to retain knowledge of all food related liked & dislikes, and manage menus accordingly. Microwave training provided.

Artwork by Katrina Simeck

Writing your hopes and wishes from a view other than your own adds a new twist on your basic journaling. Like all mothers, Katrina wishes she had more hands and more hours. Instead of writing about all she does during the day and lamenting that she needs help, she wrote her wants in the form of a kitschy "help wanted" ad. Her words are just as effective and her voice is just as authentic, but the creative approach gives the page more life and personality.

Supplies: Cardstock; brads, letter stickers, patterned paper (American Crafts)

the SURVIVAL guide

How To Survive Three Weeks in a Foreign Country With Only the Clothes on Your Back

Travel to a foreign country is unpredictable at best, no matter how well you plan. But in this installment of The Survival Guide, I will tell you how to survive three weeks in the South American country of Ecuador – and visit three different climate regions – with only the clothes on your back and the contents of your carry-on.

First, it helps to leave the States for Ecuador during the winter months. That way, you will be guaranteed to have a few layering pieces. I recommend wearing a pair of jeans, comfortable walking shoes (a must when dealing with Miami airport anyway ... you never know when you'll get bad information about check-in and have to run the equivalent of a mile or more in 10 minutes or less, while dragging your carry-on), a t-shirt, a long sleeved shirt, and a jacket. These will end up being the basis of your wardrobe for the next three weeks.

Secondly, it will benefit you to stay with a family with members of your general size and gender. They can offer up a few pieces of their own wardrobe to supplement your meager options.

Third, borrow from your boyfriend. This isn't always easy to do, especially if your boyfriend is a foot taller and a good 30 pounds heavier than you. But you'll just have to make it work.

Fourth, be prepared to wash your two t-shirts (one from your trip, one borrowed from the aforementioned boyfriend), your one pair of underwear, and your two pairs of shorts (borrowed again from the boyfriend and his mother) daily.

Fifth, it helps, when visiting the coastal region, to not be squeamish about wearing someone else's bathing suit.

Sixth, when traveling to a foreign country with only the clothes on your back, and especially if you are traveling over the Christmas holiday to visit a family who are missionaries and lead church services several times a week, in the name of all things good and holy, pack a dress in your carry-on! Even if you think this is like the dumbest idea ever, trust me: you need that dress, and you will impress your future mother-in-law to no end that you had the foresight to put that dress in your backpack.

And finally, don't be shocked to hear that your luggage will likely never reappear. Even if you and your future father-in-law stalk the airport daily to check for updates on the status of the suitcase, be prepared for the idea that you will never again see the bulk of your summer wardrobe.

Also, when you fill out a claim to be reimbursed for the value of the suitcase and its contents, lie to your mother about how much you will be receiving. Because she just might take half to replace a chartreuse green suitcase that is 30 years old, and you'll be left with barely enough to buy the necessary items to clothe yourself once again when warm weather comes.

But that leads to a whole other volume in the Survival Guide series.

Michele Skinner is a writer and reluctant traveler from Minneapolis, Minnesota. She writes these tips from experience.

What better way to journal a lot of information than to write in the form of a magazine article? It's a great way to hit all the main points and avoid text that is dry and wordy. Articles can be livened up with humor and insight in a way that basic journaling just can't. "The Survival Guide" is a result of my experience with lost luggage. Straight journaling could have sounded boring, but writing an article allowed me to share my "lessons learned" in a light-hearted, reader-friendly way.

Supplies: Cardstock (Bazzill, WorldWin); patterned paper (Autumn Leaves, Scenic Route); chipboard letters (Cosmo Cricket); rub-on letters (American Crafts); Misc: American Typewriter and Times New Roman fonts

1987, Summer: Michele was in seventh grade. Marc was in eighth grade. Michele lived in a small town in Indiana. Marc lived in South America, but was spending a year in Indiana while his family was on furlough from the mission field. Michele and her friend Erin were paddle-boating on the lake where Michele's grandparents lived. Marc and his friend Matt were shooting turtles with a BB gun on the same lake. Erin knew Matt from school and said, "Hey! I know him! Let's go flirt … he has a friend for you!" The girls paddle-boated near the boys, giggling and trying to look cute. The boys ignored them and ran off to find a quieter area for turtle-shooting. The girls got bored and paddled away.

1991, Summer: Michele worked at the dining commons of the local college. Marc got a job as a dishwasher at the same dining commons. They were introduced to each other by Rollin, a mutual friend. Michele and Marc said hello. Marc quit two weeks later.

1991, Fall: Michele's mom took a course at the local college. She came home one night and told Michele, "There's this boy in my class. He's not much of a talker, and he's from somewhere in South America, but his name is Marc, and you two would make the most beautiful babies." Michele rolled her eyes.

1992, Fall. Michele decided, against her better judgment, to attend the local college. While at the street party on the eve of the school year, she bumped into her friend, Rollin. He asked her, "Have you met my roommate, Marc?" Michele and Marc looked at each other, and both remembered meeting at the dining commons the previous year. They said hello. The boys walked away, and Michele walked away with her friend.

1993, Winter. Michel and Marc have been friends for several months. They hung out with the same people and ate meals at the same table. One day in January, proverbial lightning hit Michele and she realized, "Hey … this is a pretty cute guy. And he's actually nice. Huh." She began to obsess. And Marc began to sit by Michele in Sociology class.

1993, Spring. After three months of sitting by each other in Sociology class and getting more familiar with each other, Michele decided she really liked this Marc guy. She talked to her friend, April, who is now dating Rollin, Marc's roommate. April urged Michele to call Marc, because he was not into anything other than computers and basketball, and it would never occur to him to ask out anyone. Michele called him and asked him to a floor-activity hockey game, doubling with Rollin and April. Marc said, "Okay." They had a terrible time. Michele was non-plussed. She tried again: "Want to go to a floor activity at the skating rink?" Marc said, "Okay." They had a better time.

Michele and Marc started to spend more time together. They walked together to classes and talked afterward. They began to sit by each other at meals. But it never progressed, and Michele decided it was no longer worth the effort.

1993, Spring Break: Michele had plans to go to Myrtle Beach for the week. The day she was to leave, the phone rang. It was Marc, and he asked her to go play pool at the HUB. Surprised and pleased, Michele said, "Okay." They played pool for more than an hour, and then Michele had to leave to meet her friend and catch a Greyhound.

That night, there was a blizzard in Kentucky and the bus company canceled the trip.

Two days later, Michele bumped into Rollin and he told her Marc was home and bored, and suggested Michele call. So she did. That very day. And asked Marc if he wanted to get ice cream. He said, "Okay." They had a lovely time, and decided to meet the next morning at the college gym.

The next day, Marc and Michele had a wonderful time together. Hours flew by, and Marc admitted that he got the nerve to call Michele before spring break because he realized he would miss her and didn't want her to forget about him while she was gone. Michele smiled.

Marc walked Michele to the fine arts building where her mom worked. They walked into her office and Michele introduced Marc to her mom. Her mom looked at Marc, looked at Michele, and dragged Michele into the utility closet. "That's Handsome Marc! From my class!" Michele's mom said.

In that instant, Michele knew that she would be with Marc forever.

true — true story

love

The story of how Marc and I met takes place over several years and several missed opportunities. To capture it in a story allows it to flow much more easily than if I had just written a list of facts. For your own pages, develop a series of events into a historical narrative. Let dates or places be your chapters. Breaking up text into neat little sections makes the page easier and more fun to read.

Supplies: Cardstock (Bazzill); flower border, patterned paper (Doodlebug); letter stickers (Provo Craft); chipboard letters (Making Memories); chipboard hearts (Heidi Grace); border punch (EK Success); Misc: Goudy Old Style and ILS Script fonts, glitter, ink

GAME TIME

Operation: Delta Get to Trouble Master

For 2 Players, Ages 5 & Up
(Unless you are playing Henry Skinner, in which case this game could be played at age 3)

Object: Be the first player to complete a series of board games

Contents: 1 – Chutes & Ladders Game
           1 – CandyLand Game
           1 – Guess Who Game
           1 – Trouble Game

Set-Up: Place game boards in successive order, from Chutes & Ladders to CandyLand to Guess Who to Trouble. Place all game pieces in their starting position. Defer rolling to choose who goes first, since the youngest player will ultimately want to start the game.

To Play: Both players start playing Chutes & Ladders. The first person to complete that game then moves on to CandyLand. At the conclusion of each game, the player moves on to the next game. If one player moves on, the other player cannot leave their current game until it has been finished. When the first player gets to Guess Who, the other player must answer the questions of identity, but cannot ask their own questions until they reach the game.

To Win: Play is over when the first player completes all four games. The winner then becomes Supersonic Delta Trouble Master.

(Unless you are playing against Henry Skinner, in which case he will win and become the Supersonic Master.)

One day during summer vacation, when we were bored and stuck indoors, I got the idea to blend several games together and play them as one big game. Henry was thrilled, and we had a ball together. But instead of journaling about it in a normal way, I decided to turn the idea of the game into a manual, complete with all the headers that you find on game instructions. Looking at your story from a new perspective can give it so many new possibilities: recipe, manual, care instructions, anything with steps or descriptions can turn ordinary into extraordinary.

Supplies: Cardstock (Bazzill); patterned paper (American Crafts, Daisy D's); chipboard letters (American Crafts); chipboard accents (K&Co.); Misc: Century Gothic font

CONTRIBUTORS

CATHERINE FEEGEL-ERHARDT

I'm Catherine ... middle aged, vertically challenged, horizontally gifted mother of three with the most supportive and understanding "DH" ever! I have always had to have something busy in my hands since I can remember. In elementary school I made pencil cases out of old denim jeans and sold them ... until the nuns shut down my "business." In 2005, my son was about to advance to Eagle rank in the Boy Scouts and he "needed" a scrapbook of his scouting accomplishments. I remember the day I stepped foot into The Scrapbook Shoppe and it was love at first sight! I've had layouts published in *Paper Kuts, Memory Makers* magazine and several Memory Makers idea books. I also hold the honor of being a Memory Makers Master class of 2007! I've traveled the country taking classes and reuniting with wonderful friends who I have met over the past three years because of this passion. That has to be the best part of it all ... the friendships forged and maintained. My goals in life include learning how to play the drums and driving an 18-wheeler.

NISA FIIN

I am 28 and I live in St. Paul, Minnesota. I have a dreamy husband named Ben, a nudey pup named Hooper, three toasters (why???), a ridiculous number of hoodies, a pretty serious cranberry juice addition and a crazy messy scrap room. I am a photographer—mostly of kids and families. I love it. I'm a dork. I enjoy talking to strangers. I can always find a way to justify buying more books. I can't stand to sleep with my feet covered. I only sing in the car. And then really loud. To really loud music.

NICOLE HARPER

I began scrapbooking shortly after the birth of my only child, Allison, in 1999. After a five-year hiatus, I rediscovered my love for getting my family's story recorded, and have immersed myself ever since. I have been told that my journaling is an accurate reflection of myself—heartfelt, honest and simply real. I believe that the story is the start of any project, and without journaling that story is incomplete. It's what I want my family to remember for years to come and what I want to remember for myself that guides my work. I have been published in *Memory Makers, Creating Keepsakes, Simple Scrapbooks, Scrapbook Trends* and several idea books.

CRYSTAL JEFFREY RIEGER

I've always been interested in art, something I trained in for years before moving on to the world of fashion. After my son was born, I decided to stay home and when the need for creativity set in, I went in search of something to do. There was scrapbooking and it was love at first sight! A year later I was selected as a 2007 Memory Makers Master and have been happily creating and writing for Memory Makers ever since. In fact, Memory Makers published my first book, *Cut Loose*—very exciting!—in 2008. You can check out my blog at www.memorymakersmagazine.com/crystaljeffreyrieger. I spend my days with my husband and two kids on a beautiful horse farm in Canada.

KATRINA SIMECK

I am a mom, a wife, a friend, a businesswoman, a coffee addict, a poor housekeeper, a decent cook, and … a scrapbooker. I started scrapbooking over a decade ago, but quickly put my deco scissors down when I realized that I'd never be "caught up." When I started scrapping again a few years ago, I did it with the intention that I would scrap with a purpose. I had things to say. Stories to tell. Photos to share. My scrapbooks reflect my voice. I use sarcasm, humor, honesty … and far too many ellipses.

SANDRA STEPHENS

I love to travel. After a trip to Paris in 1998 and 32 rolls of film in my carry-on luggage, my best friend convinced me I needed to buy a scrapbook. I had no idea scrapbooking would be so fun and give me the creative outlet I craved. I now have two kids to scrap about and, of course, my travels. My husband and I escape for a couple of weeks once a year and I love it!

SUE THOMAS

While I've always been one to journal, it took a lot of persuasion to get me to try scrapbooking. I never thought I was "artistic." In 2002 when I was embarrassed enough about pulling out a plastic grocery bag of wedding photos, I finally agreed to try scrapbooking to get our wedding photos in an album. I was hooked immediately. In addition to being blessed with some incredible scrapbook-based friendships, I have had the privilege of being named to the Creating Keepsakes Hall of Fame as well as a Memory Makers Master runner up and have had a number of layouts published in various magazines and idea books. When I'm not scrapping, I spend my time practicing special education law, taking photos, driving Andrea, my daughter, to and from dance or violin, playing with our dogs and cats and going on Wednesday night dinner and Sunday morning coffee dates with my husband, Greg.

SOURCE GUIDE

The following companies manufacture products featured in this book. Please check your local retailers to find these materials, or go to a company's Web site for the latest product. In addition, we have made every attempt to properly credit the items mentioned in this book. We apologize to any company that we have listed incorrectly, and we would appreciate hearing from you. Companies with an asterisk (*) after their name generously donated product toward the creation of the artwork in this book.

7gypsies
(877) 749-7797
www.sevengypsies.com

A2Z Essentials
(419) 663-2869
www.geta2z.com

Adornit/Carolee's Creations
(435) 563-1100
www.adornit.com

All My Memories
(904) 482-0092
www.allmymemories.com

American Crafts
(801) 226-0747
www.americancrafts.com

Anchor Paper
(800) 652-9755
www.anchorpaper.com

Anna Griffin, Inc.
(888) 817-8170
www.annagriffin.com

Arctic Frog
www.arcticfrog.com

Artistic Scrapper - no source available

Autumn Leaves
(800) 588-6707
www.autumnleaves.com

Avery Dennison Corporation
(800) 462-8379
www.avery.com

BamPop LLC
www.bampop.com

BasicGrey
(801) 544-1116
www.basicgrey.com

Bazzill Basics Paper
(480) 558-8557
www.bazzillbasics.com

Berwick Offray, LLC
(800) 237-9425
www.offray.com

BoBunny Press
(801) 771-4010
www.bobunny.com

ChartPak
www.chartpak.com

Chatterbox, Inc.
(208) 461-5077
www.chatterboxinc.com

CherryArte
(212) 465-3495
www.cherryarte.com

Clearsnap, Inc.
(888) 448-4862
www.clearsnap.com

Cloud 9 Design
(866) 348-5661
www.cloud9design.biz

Collage Press
(435) 676-2039
www.collagepress.com

Colorbök, Inc.
(800) 366-4660
www.colorbok.com

Colorbox - see Clearsnap

Cosmo Cricket
(800) 852-8810
www.cosmocricket.com

Crafter's Workshop, The
www.thecraftersworkshop.com

Crate Paper
(801) 798-8996
www.cratepaper.com

Creative Imaginations
(800) 942-6487
www.cigift.com

Cross-My-Heart-Cards, Inc.
(888) 689-8808
www.crossmyheart.com

Daisy D's Paper Company
(888) 601-8955
www.daisydspaper.com

Darice, Inc.
(866) 432-7423
www.darice.com

DecoArt Inc.
(800) 367-3047
www.decoart.com

Dèjá Views/C-Thru Ruler
(800) 243-0303
www.dejaviews.com

Delta Creative, Inc.
(800) 423-4135
www.deltacreative.com

Deluxe Designs - no longer in business

Designer Digitals
www.designerdigitals.com

Diamond Dust - no source available

Die Cuts With A View
(801) 224-6766
www.diecutswithaview.com

Digital Design Essentials
www.digitaldesignessentials.com

Doodlebug Design Inc.
(877) 800-9190
www.doodlebug.ws

Dove of the East
www.doveoftheeast.com

EK Success, Ltd.
www.eksuccess.com

Every Jot and Tittle
www.everyjotandtittle.etsy.com

Fancy Pants Designs, LLC
(801) 779-3212
www.fancypantsdesigns.com

Fiskars, Inc.
(866) 348-5661
www.fiskars.com

Fontwerks
(604) 942-3105
www.fontwerks.com

Hambly Screenprints
(800) 707-0977
www.hamblyscreenprints.com

Heidi Grace Designs, Inc.
(866) 347-5277
www.heidigrace.com

Heidi Swapp/Advantus Corporation
(904) 482-0092
www.heidiswapp.com

Imagination Project, Inc.
(888)477-6532
www.imaginationproject.com

Imaginisce
(801) 908-8111
www.imaginisce.com

Impress Rubber Stamps
(206) 901-9101
www.impressrubberstamps.com

It Takes Two
(800) 331-9843
www.ittakestwo.com

Jenni Bowlin
www.jennibowlin.com

Jo-Ann Stores
www.joann.com

JudiKins
(310) 515-1115
www.judikins.com

Junkitz - no longer in business

K&Company
(888) 244-2083
www.kandcompany.com

Karen Foster Design
(801) 451-9779
www.karenfosterdesign.com

KI Memories
(972) 243-5595
www.kimemories.com

Knock Knock/Who's There, Inc.
(800) 656-5662
www.knockknock.biz

Kreinik
(800) 537-2166
www.kreinik.com

Lasting Impressions for Paper, Inc.
(800) 936-2677
www.lastingimpressions.com

Making Memories
(801) 294-0430
www.makingmemories.com

Mara-Mi, Inc.
(800) 627-2648
www.mara-mi.com

Mark Richards Enterprises, Inc.
(888) 901-0091
www.markrichardsusa.com

Martha Stewart Crafts
www.marthastewartcrafts.com

Marvy Uchida/ Uchida of America, Corp.
(800) 541-5877
www.uchida.com

May Arts
(800) 442-3950
www.mayarts.com

Maya Road, LLC
(877) 427-7764
www.mayaroad.com

Me & My Big Ideas
(949) 583-2065
www.meandmybigideas.com

Melissa Frances/Heart & Home, Inc.
(888) 616-6166
www.melissafrances.com

Michaels Arts & Crafts
(800) 642-4235
www.michaels.com

Mustard Moon
(763) 493-5157
www.mustardmoon.com

My Mind's Eye, Inc.
(800) 665-5116
www.mymindseye.com

October Afternoon
www.octoberafternoon.com

Offray- see Berwick Offray, LLC

Paper Loft, The
(801) 254-1961
www.paperloft.com

Paper Moons
www.paper-moons.com

Paper Salon
(800) 627-2648
www.papersalon.com

Paper Source
(888) 727-3711
www.paper-source.com

Paper Studio
(480) 557-5700
www.paperstudio.com

Pebbles Inc.
(801) 235-1520
www.pebblesinc.com

Piggy Tales
(702) 755-8600
www.piggytales.com

Prima Marketing, Inc.
(909) 627-5532
www.primamarketinginc.com

Provo Craft
(800) 937-7686
www.provocraft.com

PSX Design
www.sierra-enterprises.com/psxmain.html

Purple Onion Designs
www.purpleoniondesigns.com

Queen & Co.
(858) 613-7858
www.queenandcompany.com

QuicKutz, Inc.
(888) 702-1146
www.quickutz.com

Ranger Industries, Inc.
(800) 244-2211
www.rangerink.com

Reminisce Papers
(319) 358-9777
www.shopreminisce.com

Sandylion Sticker Designs
(800) 387-4215
www.sandylion.com

Sanford Corporation
(800) 323-0749
www.sanfordcorp.com

Sassafras Lass
(801) 269-1331
www.sassafraslass.com

Scenic Route Paper Co.
(801) 542-8071
www.scenicroutepaper.com

Scrapworks, LLC
(801) 363-1010
www.scrapworks.com

SEI, Inc.
(800) 333-3279
www.shopsei.com

Sharpie - see Sanford

Sonburn, Inc.
(800) 436-4919
www.sonburn.com

Stampin' Up!
(800) 782-6787
www.stampinup.com

Stemma/Masterpiece Studios
www.masterpiecestudios.com

Strano Designs
(508) 888-3189
www.stranodesigns.com

Target
www.target.com

Technique Tuesday, LLC
(503) 644-4073
www.techniquetuesday.com

Tsukineko, Inc.
(800) 769-6633
www.tsukineko.com

Two Peas in a Bucket
(888) 896-7327
www.twopeasinabucket.com

Uniball
(800) 323-0749
www.uniball-na.com

Urban Lily
www.urbanlily.com

We R Memory Keepers, Inc.
(801) 539-5000
www.weronthenet.com

WorldWin Papers
(888) 834-6455
www.worldwinpapers.com

Wrights Ribbon Accents
(877) 597-4448
www.wrights.com

Wübie Prints
(888) 256-0107
www.wubieprints.com

Zig/Kuretake Co. Ltd.
www.kuretake.co/jp

Zsiage, LLC
(718) 224-1976
www.zsiage.com

INDEX

FOR MORE INSPIRATION AND IDEAS FOR SCRAPBOOKING YOUR STORY, CHECK OUT THESE OTHER SELECTIONS FROM MEMORY MAKERS BOOKS.

Modern Memory Keeper

Celebrate the generations who have shaped your life as well as family memories in the making. With unique ideas for showcasing all kinds of family photos, you'll learn to create modern heritage keepsakes.

ISBN-13: 978-1-59963-019-9
ISBN-10: 1-59963-019-2
paperback
128 pages
Z1760

Scrapbooking Your Faith

Stir your spiritual consciousness and be inspired to create belief-based pages of your own. Whatever your spiritual journey is, this book is a treasure you'll return to again and again.

ISBN-13: 978-1-59963-002-1
ISBN-10: 1-59963-002-8
paperback
128 pages
Z0690

We Dare You

Take your art to a new level and explore new themes with the mix of thoughtful, evocative and funny Dares from authors Kristina Contes, Meghan Dymock, Nisa Fiin and Genevieve Simmonds.

ISBN-13: 978-1-59963-013-7
ISBN-10: 1-59963-013-3
paperback
128 pages
Z1041

What About the Words?

Journaling on your scrapbook layouts is easy with the advice, examples and inspirations found here.

ISBN-13: 978-1-892127-77-8
ISBN-10: 1-892127-77-6
paperback
128 pages
Z0017

These books and other fine Memory Makers titles are available at your local scrapbook retailer, bookstore or from online suppliers, or visit our Web site at www.memorymakersmagazine.com or www.mycraftivity.com